Chad Gaines

Who Am I?

You can also get signed copies of this book only from my website.

www.gaineschad.com

Also be sure to follow us on social media for more about this book and upcoming movie:

IG @gaineschad

Facebook/chadgaines

Youtube/chadgaines

Twitter/Gaineschad

Acknowledgments

When writing such a book based on one's life, there are always many to thank. I have had so many pour so much into me. God has produced something inside of my spirit that is unbreakable. I thank God for everything. His mercy upon my life has carried me from the dark to the light. So many friends have believed in me as my world and life were falling apart; thank you for your love, compassion, and strength.

For the Universities, Middle and High Schools, Churches, Juvenile Justice Centers, Companies, and Groups nationwide that have invited me to speak and share my insight and testimony. I'm not the inspiration; you are. I am honored.

Team Gaines: thank you to your devoted fans worldwide who travel to hear about my life on stages in many cities and on social media. I truly love you. Margaret and Bob Davis: For showing a scared little, lonely boy peace and manners. You are so missed every day. I thank God for sending you both to me so many years ago. I know now if you were both still here, you would say, "Thank God he sent you to us." That's just who you were as caring people.

To our friends and fans who continue to follow and support us worldwide: Christina Baxter, Dustin and Cori Meid, Bo Smith, Jason Marshall, and the late John Boren.

To the friends who helped me grow in so many ways: Joshua Beasley, RIP brother. For my wife, *Tina Yan*, for holding my hand through everything we go through. Words do not explain the love I have for you. I love you always.

Author's Note

You know, I almost didn't write this book. I almost gave up and walked away from everyone and everything. Throughout this journey, I cried. I sat on the end of my bed for hours at a time, staring out the window into the street and writing this book and detailing the outline for a featured film. I seriously wanted to take my own life after reliving this horrific story. But, what helped me move forward and not stop is that I realized later in my life that this book and this project weren't about me. It's more about you: the readers, the friends, and the family and where they can relate.

My life has been tragic yet triumphant in so many ways. This is a work of nonfiction. I have truly rendered the events of my life faithfully just as I have recalled them. Some names, actions, locations, and descriptions of individuals have been changed to remain and respect their privacy. While these circumstances, conversations, and events illustrate abuse, drug use, and alcoholism, I do not condone using any of those products or those actions in my own life.

However, all of those have been a part of life that produced who I have become as an adult business trainer and speaker today. This work is told in a way that evokes my real feelings and meanings of those times of the past. What was said and what actions came to pass. In keeping with the actual fundamental nature of the mood and spirit of those moments that shaped my life, I have used adult words I do not use now. I must warn you that this work has adult language and graphic abuse. Follow at your own risk and pace.

...based on horrific true events

For Nora....

may the winds of life be at your back and the ocean be your friend.
I love you.

Table of Contents

Who Am I?

Honolulu 2022

From the eleven-floor balcony in my hotel room, I can see the clear blue Pacific Ocean just across the street and all its beauty. In my five decades of life here on earth, I'm learning that where you start doesn't have to be where you end up. I had to come to terms with many things, people, and demons to write my story for millions.

In fact, I didn't want to do it. I couldn't talk about all the *horrible* things that happened back then. Also, I didn't want to face the embarrassment of the things that I did either. But, the many great people in my life helped me understand "this would help so many."

So, I stepped out of my comfort zone and started writing a book based on my life after months of going back and forth between opening this document, typing a few lines, to sitting in a room with movie directors in Los Angeles. My peers always told me when I was much younger that you need money to make money. I found that not to be true. No matter where you are right now in life or what you do for work, in a blink of an eye, life can change, and you could be on a different path.

Let me explain where I came from and how I even got to the sandy beaches here in Hawaii. The 1970s was the ground floor of disco music, hippies, and marijuana on the shores of California. About the time of my birth in 1973, the Vietnam War consumed the national news. Born during the war impacted the United States economy and took a mental toll on many. The death toll from the costly and lengthy conflict in Vietnam would take the lives of 3 million people, including 58,000 Americans.

In the summer of 1973, my parents birthed me into the world: my mother, Connie Gaines, and my dad, Richard Gaines. I was born at 11:34 a.m. in a town about thirty minutes east of our home in *Kewanna, Indiana.* Kewanna, Indiana, had a population of just 514 people in the 1970s. My mother was a waitress at the local truck stop. Which only made sense because my father was a cross-country truck driver. He would make three trips a week from here in *Indiana* to *New York City* delivering chocolate candy bars.

There is a certain balance between structure and passion. As a young boy, I had passion. However, I had no structure to guide me through my youth. For most of you reading *my story* for the first time, my name is Chad Gaines. I've been around here for five decades now. Let me explain what I'm trying to say to all of you. My first name is Chad. It means warrior and protector. My middle name is Richard. It means powerful or brave and was given to me by my dad. In that summer of 1973, my last name given was Gaines. The name Gaines came from the Romans and was eventually passed on to my dad in April 1944.

If you put my name together, it means a powerful Roman warrior and protector. I've heard from many friends and family that everyone has a purpose here on earth. Many people would say there is a place you're supposed to be here on earth. Some even have said everyone has a story. The difference is in those things that I have found in my life; it's harder for me to find structure and easier to find passion. So, I finally sat down to write this story back in 2019.

My story was written for you. If you can use a part of my life to help yourself, please do it! Please email us your story if you can relate to how mine was then and how it is now. This is my story written in detail as I remember it.

I think as a little boy, all I wanted to do was live. I always had a bigger picture of the world. Maybe that was that passion I spoke about earlier. Maybe it was something else.

No Structure

I'm five years old. I'm sitting in my highchair eating. My little head is pouring with sweat from the Indiana sun. Our tiny trailer is heating up like a boiling tin can. The sound of breaking glass has almost become normal in our home, even at the age of five. My mother feeds me lunch while she and my dad argue back and forth out of control. My dad sits across the table with his cigarette hanging from his mouth, shaking his head in disgust. He's drinking a can of *Budweiser* as he had always had. He's drunk and talking loudly. Even at this age, I had started to witness the beginning of a destructive cycle from yelling at each other at the kitchen table to throwing objects at one another.

In the distance, I hear Tiny Dancer by *Elton John* being broadcast on our local radio. Those words that poisoned my mother's tongue in the mid-1970s did not simply originate from her. She was educated on hate by her parents. In turn, she showed me the same hate that her parents taught her. Chances were, I would continue with our generational curse.

I discovered that at age five, I think. Those young moments when you're too young to understand but just old enough to feel something was wrong. My parents greatly lacked education. They lacked skills. They lacked goals. The one single thing they didn't lack was work ethic. My mother had put in many hours working on her feet at the local truck stop. My dad was a cross-country truck driver. He was then around 6' tall. By 1978, my dad had spent time in and out of jail for fighting and drinking. My mother was much shorter at 5'6 and didn't drink or smoke. That was my foundation as a young boy growing up in the 1970s.

Classic cars, the music, the clothes, and the friends. The last of the American soldiers were leaving the Vietnam War. Our nation's 37th President was Richard Nixon. The President announced the United States had 45,958 combat fatalities in the Vietnam War. The following summer, I would turn six years old. That summer was incredible! My dad was working less and less due to America's *ongoing inflation* problem. I felt so alive that summer, if that's even possible for a 6-year-old. It was fun and full of laughs.

The fishing trips with my dad are what I remember. I remember on a Saturday morning, after watching cartoons and having a bowl of Captain Crunch, we would walk down to the pond to *go fishing*. I held that Scooby Doo fishing pole like it was a trophy. My dad always had a *cigarette* hanging out of his mouth and a *beer* in his right hand while we were fishing. On the other hand, my mother was dressed in sweatpants and had a mouth full of poison toward others. She spends most of the day fighting and arguing with others on the house *phone*. My trip down to the pond with my dad that day would forever impact my life and how I trust people, even *four decades* later.

After Saturday morning cartoons, we would walk down to the pond, meet with *Claude Wagoner*, joke, and fish to pass the time. I would wear my bib overalls like Claude's. He would pick on me with bullfrogs by putting them in my pocket, and he and my dad would laugh as I hopped around with a bullfrog in my pocket.

It was a hot Indiana summer day in July of 1979. Often, I would stay at the *pond* and fish with Claude as my dad would drive into town to get food and his cigarettes. I was about a month away from entering the first grade then. Little did I know, our morning fishing trip would eventually go on into the evening. My dad was still gone hours after he left for the town. Finally, the day slowly turned into night, and Claude decided to walk me home and back to my mother. A few days later, I was told that my dad had gone on a trip and was never returning home. The news shook me.

After my dad left, things dramatically changed. As a result of his absence, I developed some emotional and parenting skills. Unfortunately, however, these were accompanied by abusive put-downs and blood-curdling beatings from my mother.

"You dumb little son of a bitch" "You're just like your lazy ass, good for nothing dad" "You're never going to amount to shit Chad!"

With every hateful word and every physical slap from my mother, I began to retreat inside myself. I retreated even further inside myself while at school to empty and lonely darkness. In addition, with every retreat and silence, the armored wall inside of me grew thicker and became less penetrable over time as a young boy. I was taught that violence solved every problem in my life. As a young boy, I lived minute to minute. I always wondered to what measure or degree this would lead. One little event always leads to more significant events of abuse.

My mother always felt comfortable humiliating me in those days by always yelling. Sometimes, things went as far as backhands across my face that eventually grew completely out of control at home. Her anger was more like a dictatorship than a parent caring for their only child. Making my lips bleed from all the backhands was not enough for my mother. She would call me unbearable words or spit into my face while yelling and beating me across my lower back and legs with the brown leather belt. She would say that the belt was used as some kind of weapon to keep me under control.

"You little cock sucker, I'll fucking kill you before the day ends!"

When you have the time as a child to prepare to get hit, you learn fast what part of the body to protect. I would always wear two pairs of pants to protect myself from the welts from the leather belt. The tears ran down my red cheeks onto my lips as I sat on my bedroom floor, broken and sick to my stomach.

My behavior became that of a self-destructive boy. When my mother realized the leather belt was no longer a force against me, other games were played to control and break the strength of my mind as well as my body. My mother would re-emerge into my bedroom from the living room. My bedroom door would virtually be torn off the hinges from her impact. I often thought, "What new craze will she unleash against my seven-year-old body?" The blows repeatedly came from every direction, like a prizefighter in the middle of the ring. My head remained looking straight down toward the brown shag carpet that lay in my bedroom, hoping not to provoke her wrath any further.

The blood ran from the sides of my swollen mouth as Mother's backhands continued again from every direction. She then grabbed my little body by my blond hair, threw me onto my bed, and then locked the door on her way out. I lay there completely covered in blood from the blows to my mouth and head area. I felt my spirit leave my body. She must have killed me, I thought.

About ten minutes later, I heard my mother ramble back down the hallway toward my bedroom. Mother returned in a completely different tone and with a completely different character. "What was she thinking?" I thought to myself. Does she even realize what she did to her only son ten minutes ago? From that night on, I knew something was wrong with my living situation. I knew that my mother was mentally ill due to something. But unfortunately, I was just too young to understand what it was.

That night, we left the house to eat dinner. As we passed most of the restaurants on the city's edge, I realized that the little joy I had about going out had turned into horror. I trembled with fear. It's like one of those times in your life you can feel something terribly wrong, but you just can't put your finger on it. My mother's curse words rolled from her tongue as her dirty breath filled the car. Our car drove down that old country road with pure passion, from that big old engine to that loud muffler tied up with clothes hangers.

Our car, a yellow 1977 Oldsmobile Cutlass or "the rust bucket," as her few friends named it, was our little piece of paradise for traveling in the late 1970s. She turned left along another country road. I felt certain this might be where they would ultimately find my broken body. I envisioned the phone call she would make to police officials, explaining how there was a terrible accident and how her child fell out of the car.

I sat in the front seat of "the rust bucket," shrugged my shoulders, and replied, "Ok Mom, you are the boss," telling her what she always liked to hear from her son.

By this time, our car was turning into Margaret and Bob's driveway. As the car came to a loud thunderous crash from the motor and a single backfire from the dirty muffler held by my mother's clothes hangers, we arrived at our location. I was laughing hysterically on the inside while dying on the outside. My mother's detachment from reality was a much-needed comic relief for me. She had no idea of the happiness Margaret and Bob gave me.

Margaret and Bob Davis were in their late 70s in the early 1980s. What incredible people they both were. They were married twenty years before, in the mid-1960s. Bob served in the United States military during World War II. In the late 1970s, Bob worked as a foundry worker until he retired. Margaret Davis was a stay-at-home wife who worked on building and sewing blankets as she ran her daycare right from their house. Margaret never gave birth to any children. She cared for many little children, including me, when my mother had enough of slapping me around.

I always enjoyed the freedom from my mother when I was visiting Margaret and Bob's home. Honestly, I have never met two people on this planet who cared more for children than they did. They saved my life many times through my younger years without even knowing it. The Davis' saved me from the pain and insults carried out by my mother at home. They showed me deep peace for the first time in my short life.

After discovering my home's physical and emotional abuse, Margaret and Bob took their biggest gamble and closed down their home daycare to take care of me. The more I visited, the more my mother allowed me the freedom to stay longer and longer.

As I entered second grade, for the second time due to missing school because of the physical abuse, I noticed that I was spending more time night after night at the Davis' home. My mother was frequently away and, during those times, had the Davis' take care of me. I never understood the times when my mother would disappear. There were times it was for days and other times for weeks. I could never make sense of the whole situation as to whether she was out binge drinking or off with a new boyfriend for a while. Nevertheless, I welcomed that break while at the Davis' from all the abuse from my mother.

Once she was back, the mental and physical abuse continued. One morning, I sat at our kitchen table with food running down my chin after hearing my mother call for me like a drill sergeant. I thought to myself, how far away was the front door? I thought to myself, could I make it out? I managed to slide my legs out from underneath the table and stood on my feet to face my fate.

I entered my bedroom with my head straight down, looking at the old brown carpet in my bedroom, hoping again not to provoke Mother's rage. Mother started to yell into my face right before knocking me upside my head. The blood ran from the gums of my mouth as the backhands continued to come from what seemed to be every direction. Mother then grabbed me by the hair, threw me onto my bed, and locked the door on her way out. As I lay there completely covered in blood from the blows to my mouth, I was determined to live and not let her win this war.

Some of the teacher's reactions at school were kind due to my situation. They were aware of my situation but did very little to expose my family's secret of abuse. When I reentered the fourth grade for the second time in two years, the overwhelming humiliation of watching my friends go onto the fifth grade while I was held behind was devastating to me. I was physically and emotionally beaten up at home and mentally and emotionally disgraced in school. At the end of the year, after repeating the fourth grade for the second time, I was moved to the fifth grade with all D's. At that point, the teachers and the school had all but given up on the "dirty slow boy," as they named me. I had become a burden to them.

For many years, my mother lived in a cloud of depression and hurt herself. During her childhood, my mother was tormented by her appearance and the lack of education she acquired through her brief years of schooling. She only had six years of education, was abused as a child, and now left by her husband to raise me alone. At some small moments, I had seen her find peace at an amusement park we visited with her pact of friends. However, her depression would still return and haunt her.

Back at home, the beatings just kept getting worse. Soon enough, I became numb to all the pain. That was my source of learning how the world works.

Our big blue, single-story, two-bedroom home sat adjacent to Clay and 9th streets. After the events that took place during the summertime of the early 1980s, I understood as a young boy the battle wasn't between my mother and me. It was between her and her terrifying moments as a young girl. Those feelings spilled over into her adulthood, and the rage would play against me. The setup of our house was like this - through the front door was our living room. As you turn right, the first room was our bathroom, and further down the hall was Mother's room. The kitchen was off to the left of the living room. As you passed through the kitchen and stepped two steps down, you were in the center of my room. The basement steps were on the other side of the kitchen next to the back door. There is always much more going on behind the scenes of our home than the public has seen.

> *"Hating people is like burning down your own house to get rid of a rat." ~Harry Emerson Fosdick*

One evening, my mother called out my name from the bathroom. Her shift at her work was about to start soon. I stand on my feet, and my knees wobble out of fear from her voice. I walk to the doorway of our bathroom. She is looking into the mirror and rubbing makeup on her face. She turns toward me and says, "It's time for a bath." I lean in and turn both knobs. My mother tells me that her shift will start soon and that I need to hurry it up. I thought to myself peace would be on my side in about an hour.

For me, the moments in our bathroom that summer evening were a movement of unparalleled bravery and spineless actions on both our parts. I referred to it then as "God's angels in the bathroom." I didn't see it coming; I wasn't ready. The truth is, how could I have known? I was just eight years old, 55 pounds if I was lucky. My mother always used this weird, long, silver thing to twist her hair into curls. It looked like a magic trick. She would plug it into the outlet in the bathroom, and in fifteen minutes, her hair was in big, long curls.

I stepped out of my one-piece, zipped to the neck pajamas. I was still standing, waiting for the tub to fill as Mother stared into the fogged mirror. She laughs at how skinny I am and how I look in front of her. She says loudly, "I can't believe something like you came from me!" She shakes her head in disgust over the way I look. I am defenseless at that point. Even at that age, I knew that I had to position myself closer to the doorway in case this turned dangerous for me and I had to escape. She stood between me and my only way out. I just kept staring at the tub and the water hoping not to infuriate

9

her in any way possible. To keep her appeased, I tried to laugh with her at myself. I thought if I accepted that she was right and I was just worthless and ugly, nothing bad would happen.

I filled the tub with bubbles as she rumbled about how I was just like my worthless, no-good dad. She called me "Chad Richard," trying to get a reaction from me. I said nothing. I know this game of hers. She then furiously turned toward me again, glared at my face, and said, "I hope to God you never have kids." The next thing I knew, she backhanded me across the face for watching her in the mirror. My legs felt weak all the way to my bones. She shoved me against the bathroom wall and held me there with her forearm against my throat.

For a moment, I felt paralyzed with shock by her quickness of anger. I gasped for a little air between her words and her arm against my neck. I thought to myself, will I get out of this mess? She reaches for the sink with one arm against me and grabs her magic curling iron. I squirm back and forth. My eyes water. Her only words were, "I'll make sure you never have kids. I'm doing this, Chad Richard, for your own good!" She ripped the curling iron from the plug-in and held it in her hand. The cords swing back and forth. She rips the towel from me, and I squirm even more, not knowing what is coming next. She commands me, "hold still damn it!" This will only take a second little boy. I cry out in pain as the curling iron burns the skin of my private areas. The torment of the curling iron touching my bare skin was like sitting on top of a furnace naked. What seemed to be long minutes were only seconds. I'm sure, however, the pain and torture were horrifying. I cried for help, which this time scared my mother, so she let go of me. I ran naked through the house. I knew Mother would finish what she had just started. At this point, I knew I might die even before I became a teenager. I heard footsteps coming through the living room toward my bedroom. I raced to put some pants on. I heard our doorbell ring, and it was her friend coming to pick my mother up for work. I heard my mother yell, "Just a minute and I'll be right out." I heard the front door slam hard, and I heard the DJ on the radio say, "This is Bobby Rivers, I'm taking you through the night." I was completely exhausted on my bed with shame and emotional pain. The next song the DJ played was Journey's, Don't Stop Believin. I don't think that was an accident.

Less than Zero

Nothing my mother did was by accident. I ran for my life during my elementary school years. By the time I was nine years old, I had found that my mother could go to work and be the nicest woman you would want to meet. However, at home, she could spit in my face and then ask me if I wanted something to eat.

I was on guard day and night, fearing what might happen next. There was just nowhere to hide from her violence. My childhood heroes were on our TV set. The beatings didn't stop with spitting and slapping. They became more brutal as I grew. Summertime break from school was the worst to go through. More time at home with my mother was more horrific than any child should have to withstand.

I didn't feel I would live long enough to make it to middle school. The attacks from my mother broke me physically, and her words broke me mentally, where I always felt *less than zero*.

The summer of 1982 was different. That summer, all of us were outside. I thought maybe, just maybe, whatever had been bothering my mother for years after Dad left our home was over. After playing a wiffle ball game in a friend's backyard, I returned home to find my mother outback grilling food on our deck. I was so relieved just to see her smile. "Hot dogs on the grill," I said loudly. But, unfortunately, this was just a set-up for the *most brutal* attack I would ever experience from my mother.

The edge of the knife was a burnt black color. My mother raised the knife in front of the grill with her right hand. She suddenly turned toward me and viciously stabbed me in the arm. I tried to defend myself. I put both hands up to say, "ok, Mother, you win!" The knife pierced into my right hand like warm butter. My blood was all over our deck. I am thinking; I can't believe my mother just killed me outside in the daytime during summer. I had a two-inch gash in my arm and another two-inch open gash on my right hand. I got away and somehow made it back into our house. I ran to lock myself in our bathroom. The event was over as fast as it had started. I was in bad shape.

My next thought was, will anyone drive me to the hospital, or will I die on the bathroom floor? After a quick phone between my mother and grandmother, I thought I would die. My grandmother told my mother she shouldn't take me to *any hospital* because there might be an investigation into what happened at our house. My mother quickly drove me to my grandmother's house so they could both bandage up my two stab injuries. They were successful, if you want to call it that. However, it would be another three weeks before the bleeding stopped from under some *cheap butterfly bandages* that my mother bought from the grocery store.

At school that year, some of my classmates questioned the injury to my arm. They ask me, what had cut me so deep. I could only come up with the excuse that the injury was caused when I wrecked my bike.

The cover-up from the abuse went on for most of my young life. Who can you tell that to and expect anyone in charge to listen? I didn't know who I could trust or talk to about what happened inside my home. At school, I kept quitting while failing every grade of school from missing nearly an average of 35-40 a year.

The thing about my mother's abuse is that it came out of nowhere. It was so random and arbitrary that I had no time to prepare. I could not even form a plan on how to prevent or skirt around her anger because anything could set her off. Anything.

One of the worst instances was because I wanted something to eat. My mother hardly ever cooked. If I told her I was hungry, she would ignore me or tell me to make something for myself. As a seven-year-old, I didn't know how to make much, but I had seen her make hot dogs enough times that I could remember the steps.

One day after school, my stomach rumbled. I padded to the kitchen in my socks to find something to eat. I was careful to wear socks in the kitchen because the floor was dirty, just like the rest of the place. The tile floor was scuffed and worn from years of not being swept or mopped. The kitchen was relatively small, just a long, narrow space with a refrigerator at the entrance. The brown, ugly cabinets at the end seldom held any dishes.

The dishes were usually dirty, piled up in the sink. Flies buzzed around them, and the smell of mildew constantly hung over the house. My mother never washed the dishes; if they were dirty, she would just let them sit in the sink until they became so bad that she would throw everything out and buy new ones. We ate on paper plates a lot.

I cast my eyes over the kitchen that day. The two-top table was just as messy as ever. Bills, coats, sweatshirts, pens, sticky notes, and various pieces of junk covered the table. We never used the table for its purpose; it was simply where discarded items were placed, gathering dust like the rest of the house.

When I opened the pantry door, I sneezed. Dust covered everything in the house, and sometimes I had trouble breathing. Only later did I realize that not everyone's house was so messy, so dirty all the time. I didn't know dishes were supposed to be cleaned and put into the dishwasher and the cabinets afterward.

That day, I looked for cereal. Sometimes I could eat cereal out of the box, but there wasn't anything that day. I walked over to the turquoise refrigerator. Nothing in the house matched anything; the furniture was different colors. Everything was out of place, from the color scheme to the piles of junk lying in the corners of the house.

I yanked on the door; my stomach rumbled loudly now. All I saw was some molded fruit, a carton of milk that I suspected was spoiled, some condiments, and a package of hot dogs. I only knew how to make hot dogs, so I took them out. I searched for a usable pan, rifling through disorganized cabinets. I scooted a chair over to the sink to fill the pan with water. I placed it on the stove, then turned the heat on high. I then ripped open the bag of hot dogs and dumped all of them in at once because that was how I had seen my mother do it. I was famished, but I knew hot dogs tasted better warm, so I waited. I would see that they were ready when the steam rose and the water boiled. All I wanted was something to eat.

When my mother entered the kitchen, I knew I had done something wrong. Her eyes narrowed to slits as they flitted from the stove to me.

"What are you doing?" she demanded.

The anger crackled around her like electricity. I would have run out the door if I had known what would happen. But I was hungry.

"Just making hot dogs," I mumbled.

She stomped to the stove. She grabbed the handle of the pot. "I told you not to touch the stove!" she screamed. Then she threw the pot of boiling water at me.

I tried to dodge, but there was no time to react. It was in horrible slow motion, like a dream, but it happened so fast, in less than a blink. The steaming water arced toward me. Hot dogs flew everywhere. Instinctively, I held up my left arm to block the boiling wave. The water hit my arms; I didn't even register the pain. Everything happened so quickly. I cried out when the water hit me, which I was afraid to do because it might make her angrier.

"I told you to never touch the fucking stove!" she yelled.

The pain shot up my arms like lightning. Instantly, I had second-degree burns, and my skin was already red, and blisters would form. It hurt so badly, but I could only stare at my mother, wondering how she could do that. Wondering what I had done was so bad that I deserved to have hot water thrown at me.

The hot dogs were strewn all over the kitchen. The pain was like thousands of angry bees stinging me simultaneously. I had no idea what to do. If I moved, that might make her more furious. If I cried, that might make her angrier.

My mother tossed the pan into the sink. She gestured to all the water and hot dogs strewn over the kitchen floor. "Clean up this fucking mess. I don't want to tell you twice."

Tears welled in my eyes. I kept my eyes on the floor as I bent down to pick up the hot dogs. However, reaching for one hurt my arm so badly that I cried out again. I was in pain and fear and all over something to eat. One of the horrible lessons of that day was that I could no longer trust anyone; all I needed was something to eat, and I was punished for it. I learned that I would be punished just for having basic human needs.

That was what hurt me more than the physical abuse: the mental abuse. I learned that having needs would lead to mind games. Would I be horribly punished for something I needed? I took a risk whenever I made myself something to eat or put on clothes, or played with my toys.

I took out the mop that we kept wedged between the wall and the fridge. I tried to mop up the water, but it hurt too much.

When my mother returned, she looked at the floor, still messy with hot dogs, and demanded, "Why haven't you cleaned this? Are you too stupid to hold a mop?"

I just held up my arm. Blisters covered my left forearm, and ugly red welts oozed liquid.

My mother just glanced at me and huffed. "Get your coat. We're going to Grandma's. Now!" she snapped.

I picked up my coat from the kitchen table but didn't put it on; it would have hurt too much. Before my mother could see me, I scooped up one of the hot dogs to eat on the way.

Once in the car, I snuck bites when my mother wasn't looking. I was in the backseat; I tried to distance my mother and myself as much as possible. We were driving down the side streets when she suddenly looked in the rearview mirror.

"Chad," she said. Her tone said *to pay attention*.

I looked up.

"What happened was an accident," she said. "An accident, do you understand?"

"An accident," I repeated dully. I glanced out the window. I imagined myself playing with toys or watching TV in one of the other houses. Somewhere else. Anywhere else.

"So when the teacher asks you what happened to your arm, you're going to say it was an accident, right?"

I didn't reply. I was in too much shock. The child that I was knew it wasn't an accident; I didn't want to lie to people, but it was something that my mother had told me many times.

"Right?" she screeched.

"Right," I mumbled.

"What are you going to say when people ask you about your arm?"

"That was an accident."

She nodded. "*Good.*"

We pulled into my grandmother's driveway, and my mother exited the car without looking at me. I opened the door, wincing because of the pain. Even though the sun was shining, I felt cold. I shivered. I hated going to my grandmother's house. It smelled like her cheap perfume, boiled eggs, and mildew, the same as my house.

My mother pounded on the door.

"What?" demanded my grandmother as she yanked open the door.

Gesturing at me, she said, "There was another accident."

My grandmother looked at the welts on my arms. "Get inside."

When the door was closed, and no one could hear, my grandmother hissed, "You sure are stupid. How could you let this happen again?"

For a second, I wasn't sure if she was talking to my mother or me.

"He was messing up the stove," replied my mother.

"You're such an idiot," my grandmother said, walking toward the bathroom. I heard her rummaging around in drawers and cabinets. She walked out with a dark brown bottle, a tube of ointment, and some bandages. "They're going to come snooping around here if you keep this up. Do you want to get arrested? Thrown in jail?" She grabbed my arm, the one that wasn't burned, and yanked me toward her. I cried out in shock.

"Shut up," she said. She dumped hydrogen peroxide on my skin, and it stung. Then, she turned to my mother, "You're so goddamn cheap. You don't have any of this in that shit hole of a house?"

My mother's only response was to chew on a fingernail and shrug.

"Goddamn cheap. Just like your father. Just like your father when he was alive." She slathered ointment on the burns, then wrapped them messily. She was not gentle. I did not know gentleness until many years later.

My grandmother examined her work. "Just don't wash it," she said. "Don't go in the shower for a few days." Then, like my mother, she pointed at me. "You know to keep your mouth shut, right?"

"What?"

"This was an accident," said my grandmother. "Do you want your mother to go to jail? Be arrested?"

If jail meant not seeing my mother for a long time, then yes, I did want that, but I sensed it was not the correct answer.

"N—no..."

"Then if anyone asks, it was an accident."

Learning To Fly

I was probably about three years old when I first started seeing Bob and Margaret. I wouldn't be here if not for them. I would be either dead or in prison. They were great and loving people who truly made a difference in my life. So few people exist like them. They ran a daycare center that my mother found an ad for in the local paper. Looking back, it was astounding that my mother trusted them enough to watch me. Not that she thought that they would hurt me; rather, my mother was always afraid of someone going to Child Protective Services or the police.

But Bob and Margaret were the sorts of people who earned your trust almost instantly. They were in their 70s when I was a child, but they still worked. They never had any children of their own, but they loved kids. They poured their hearts and souls into taking care of me.

The next day, after the incident with the boiling water, I asked my mother if I could stay over at Bob and Margaret's house. At first, it started as a once-a-month activity; then, as time passed, it turned into me staying at my house only once a month.

She didn't look at me as she was getting ready for work. "Why do you want to go out there?" she asked as if I had requested to visit a landfill.

I shrugged. I couldn't tell her how much I wanted to stay with Bob and Margaret. Otherwise, she would use that against me. "I don't know, they help me with my homework and stuff." Maybe if I presented school as a reason—instead of the toys, TV set, and delicious home cooked food—she would be more willing to say yes.

"Hm, good, you need it. Your grades are horrible, you know that? You'll end up being a dumbass."

My arm still burned underneath the bandages, and I resisted the urge to scratch. "Yeah," I said.

She flicked a hand in my direction. "Fine. Just tell her to call, like usual."

Since it was Friday, I decided to press my luck. "Can I stay the entire weekend?"

Maybe my mother felt guilty about the boiling water incident, but more than likely, she was just eager to have the house to herself and not to have to take care of a child. "Yes. They're going to spoil you, you know."

I didn't let myself smile in front of her, but inside, I beamed. I walked out the door to catch the bus. I allowed myself to smile only when the bus pulled up to the school.

As I've mentioned, school was difficult for me. Between the mental and physical abuse, I didn't have the confidence that most kids have to succeed. I didn't believe in myself, so I failed or couldn't concentrate. I tried to fade into the background and not bring attention to myself, but my teacher stopped at my desk anyway.

"Chad?" My second-grade teacher had a kind voice. She was one of the only teachers who had the patience for what she did. She squatted to be eye-level with me and gently motioned to my arm. "What happened there?"

I didn't look her in the eye. I remembered what my mother and grandmother had told me.

What if I tell the truth and my mom finds out, and I can't go to Bob and Margaret's anymore?

I was sure that would happen if I told the truth. I could see it all: my mother discovering my betrayal and cutting off all communication with Bob and Margaret.

"It was an accident," I replied.

"An accident?"

"Yeah."

I didn't elaborate.

"Well, what kind of accident?" My teacher had a kind voice, but I was scared. My knees trembled underneath my desk. I couldn't tell her the truth. Not the whole truth, anyway.

"I, um…" I didn't know how to explain. I was only eight, and eight-year-olds are not very good liars. My mother hadn't told me what to say to others when they pressed for information.

Plus, all my anger toward my mother came to the surface. It wasn't fair. I had to lie, to be a bad kid, so that I wouldn't lose Bob and Margaret. Couldn't this teacher see that I wanted her to go away?

"I said it was an accident!" I shouted. Hot tears pressed against my eyes. All of the pressure of lying was too much for a little boy. I just wanted her to leave, to stop asking questions. I kept my eyes fixed on my scuffed, dirty tennis shoes.

My teacher blinked in surprise and straightened up. "Chad, there's no shouting in class. You'll have to receive a demerit."

"Ooooo, Chad got in trouble," chimed a boy in my class.

I became even angrier. Why was I getting punished for doing what my mother told me? I was supposed to say that it was an accident.

Of course, I couldn't explain the complexities of physical and mental abuse to my teacher. All I knew was that I was so angry, and the anger didn't have anywhere to go.

"Shut up!" I yelled.

All the kids turned to stare at me, and a wave of embarrassment overtook me. Now I was the weird, troublemaking kid. All I wanted was to go to Bob and Margaret's house.

When school finally let out, I ran to the bus. I sat by myself and bounced my leg up and down all the way to their stop. When I saw Margaret's face in the window, something became looser in my chest. I didn't know why, but spending time with them felt good. I couldn't explain as a child, but their kindness and warmth helped keep me grounded.

Margaret had hired someone to install a window in her kitchen so she could watch me get on and off the bus. My mother must have called her because she was there, ready for me. I loved that about Margaret.

When I walked up to the door, I didn't even have to ring the bell. The door opened, and a warm smell enveloped me. She always made dinner early, so I wouldn't have to wait long to eat after school.

"Chad!" she greeted. I loved how she greeted me whenever I went over like I had spent years away, as if I was the best thing about her day. Her eyes went to my bandage, and her lips tightened into a thin line, but she didn't say anything at first. "Are you hungry?"

I nodded. My mother hadn't sent me to school with lunch, and I didn't have money in my cafeteria account.

"Well, come on in." She opened the door wide.

As I stepped across the threshold, I looked around. "Where's Bob?" I asked.

"Oh, he's still at the daycare. He'll be here soon. Here—" She handed me a small ham-and-cheese sandwich. "That'll hold you over til dinner."

I took a huge bite. I didn't realize how hungry I was. I ate it in about four bites.

"Wow, you polished that off," said Margaret. She patted my hand. "But then, you're a growing boy. Would you like some milk?"

I nodded. "Yes."

"Yes...?" She gave a warm smile.

"Oh. Yes, *please.*"

"Good job! I hope you've been practicing your manners at school." She shuffled to the fridge. When she came back, she handed me a cold glass.

"Thank you," I said emphatically to let her know that I was practicing.

"You're very welcome."

I hadn't known people practiced good manners until Bob and Margaret. "Please" and "Thank you" were never spoken at my mother's.

As I drank, Margaret spoke carefully. "That looks like it hurt pretty bad," she said, pointing to my arm. She didn't ask what happened.

"Um, yeah."

"Does it still hurt?"

"Kind of." I didn't want her to worry about me, so I added quickly, "But I'm OK."

Margaret paused. She knew about my mother and what she did, which is why she and Bob let me stay over so much.

"Can you tell me what happened?" she asked. Her voice was so low and kind that it was easy to trust. Still, I was afraid my mother would do something horrible if I told anyone, even Margaret.

I shook my head. "No, I'm not supposed to." I paused. "It was an accident."

Margaret nodded as if she understood everything. "Well, let's get you an extra vitamin so that it can heal. Why don't you play a little bit before dinner?"

I scooted off the chair and went downstairs. My fondest memories were playing downstairs. The downstairs of Bob and Margaret's house versus mine was like night and day. At my house, it was the dungeon, a place of fear. My mother put cardboard over the windows so I couldn't look out, and no one could look inside at what my mother might do to me. She locked me up, and I sometimes spent hours in that cold, dank basement.

But at Bob and Margaret's, everything was warm and clean. Before I started going to their house regularly, their bottom story was just a plain, cement room. However, once I stayed over more often, they put in carpet, painted the walls, and put up decorations. Bob and I sometimes worked on train sets, so there were scattered train cars. I even had a 19-inch TV all to myself, where I could watch whatever I wanted, unlike at my mother's, where she would yell at me if she wanted me to change the channel to something she liked.

I played with my Star Wars figures for a while, then carefully put them away when Margaret called for dinner. I wanted her to know I was practicing good manners so that I could come over again.

After dinner, I sat watching TV in the living room. Bob and Margaret still sat at the table. They were speaking in low voices, and I could overhear them.

"We've got to do something, Bob," said Margaret. "Did you see his arm?"

"Yes. I can't believe it. He looks like he escaped a forest fire."

"I'm afraid she'll do something worse."

"What do you want to do?"

"We need to watch him more often. What if we close down the daycare center?"

"What!" Bob cleared his throat and spoke more softly. "We can't close down the daycare center."

"We have enough in our savings account. Bob…Chad needs us."

Even though I was pretending to watch the television, I smiled. A little ball of warmth bloomed in my chest. Margaret loved me, and I could hear it in her voice.

"I know he does. But…"

"We'll make it work," said Margaret gently yet firmly. "We'll taper off, so that the parents have time to find other daycares. But Chad needs us. I can't stand it anymore. Not after what she did to him."

"What if we went to CPS?" Bob asked.

"And have them throw him into the foster system? Absolutely not," she said. "There's no guarantee that we could watch him that way."

"You're right… you're right." Bob sighed. "Let's do it."

The Will

No one in my life ever impacted me like Bob and Margaret did. No one I've known would have given up their livelihood to care for one child. They were a bright point against so much darkness. When I stayed over, we would always sit down at the table, like a normal family, which was something my mother and I never did. For breakfast, Margaret always made me a grapefruit, sprinkled sugar, and cut-out squares paired with a glass of Ovaltine and a Flintstone vitamin. Those times of normalcy made me realize how horrible conditions were at my own house.

They also led me to a discovery I wouldn't have been exposed to at home. In between learning about good manners, they also taught me about respecting people's differences, including race. My family was very vicious and violent but also very racist. We weren't supposed to be friends, talk, or hang out with "those people." Ironically, it almost drove me to want to know more and wanting to understand. Why are you saying that people of color are so bad?

Of course, it came down to treating people who are friendly as friends. Bob worked in a factory as a pipefitter with the father of a famous singer, who was Black. Bob, Margaret, and I would pile into an old station wagon a couple of times a month and meet this family at a taco spot in Gary, Indiana. We would sit around the table talking, and I couldn't understand why my mother hated non-white people so much. Everyone was open, friendly, and warm. Later I realized that it was just this false sense of insecurity that my mother and grandmother had. Growing up with Bob and Margaret helped me in many different areas of my life.

However, my time with them was cut short when I was ten.

When they started caring for me, Bob and Margaret were already in their 70s. By the time I was ten, Bob was in his 80s. They had no children, and I became their child in practice, but not legally. At the time, I didn't think they would ever die; I knew about and understood the concept of death, but I didn't think it would happen to them for a long time. It was just never a thought in my mind. It was like thinking about your favorite superhero dying; it was always a possibility, but of course, it wouldn't happen.

About the time that Bob was diagnosed with cancer, they decided to leave me everything in their will. They didn't have any other family. They explained to my mother and me what they wanted one day when my mother picked me up from their house.

My mother, of course, was in a foul mood. Something must have happened at work, or someone cut her off in traffic, or any one of the million things that could happen to make my mother angry. She was short and didn't feel like staying long. However, Bob and Margaret needed to tell us both about the will.

"Mrs. Gaines, will you come sit down?" asked Margaret.

"No," snapped my mother. "I need to leave now."

"Please?" insisted Margaret. "It's important. It concerns Chad."

My mother bristled. Were they going to tell her they finally contacted the police or CPS? "Fine."

They led us to the dining room table, where a manilla envelope lay on the surface. My mother looked so out of place in that house, and I felt uncomfortable even in the brief time she was there. It was like having a dog at a cat shelter or a trash can in the middle of the beach, something that just didn't fit.

Sitting stiffly in the chair, my mother glanced from Bob to Margaret. "Well?"

Margaret looked to Bob to start. He cleared his throat and said, "We're not going to live forever, you know. And we don't have any children of our own." He placed a hand on the manilla envelope and fidgeted with it. "This is our will. We've made several copies, and we'll give one to you and Chad both."

Margaret laid a steadying hand on Bob's arm, and he smiled softly. He then drew some papers out of the envelope. "Now, we don't have much. Just this house, the tractor, and our two cars. There's a little money in a few accounts, but…again, it's not much."

My mother sat still in her chair, and I could almost see the gears turning behind her eyes. This was not where she thought this would go; she had been on the defensive, thinking they would tell her off. Now they were talking about wills and money?

"So what does this have to do with Chad?" she asked.

"Well, when the time comes, we have specified that everything goes to him," explained Margaret. "We want to be sure…" her voice quivered at the end. "…that he's taken care of."

"You could sell the house," said Bob. "Keep the money for college. Or keep it. It's up to you, Chad." He slid a few copies of the will toward my mother and me.

Almost instantly, my mother's demeanor changed. It was as if a snake had shed its skin. She relaxed into the chair, and her voice took on a sickly sweet tone. "You're leaving Chad…everything?"

"That's right," said Margaret. "It all goes to him when we die."

I glanced up sharply. As a ten-year-old, I didn't understand fully about wills, but the word "die" caught my attention. Fear gripped my heart. Surely, it wasn't possible that they were going to die? And leave me alone with my mother?

I didn't fully comprehend what they were saying at the time about the house, cars, and money. Later, I would.

"So that's what we want," finished Bob. "We think that this is the best way. It's all there in the will."

A smile spread across my mother's face. "I understand," she said. "Everything goes to Chad."

Of course, as it was my mother, she would twist the situation for her gain.

There were a few bright spots in my life. Bob and Margaret were one of them. The other was Mark Bond. Mark was basically my only friend. Even today, I'm still friends with his dad. Mark and I did things that normal kids do: play wiffle ball, basketball and ride bikes. We loved playing basketball so much that we shoveled the basketball court free of snow at 10 pm so that we could play. We were already hot, sweaty, and tired by the time we finished, and the snowflakes fell around us, piling up where we had just shoveled.

But I loved playing on the court that night because everything was still. Peaceful. No yelling, cursing, or threat of danger. Just two boys playing together.

Mark knew what was going on with my mother. He was a very loving friend and had a lot of sympathy. He saw my mother lash out at me when it was time for me to go inside or the rare times he came over to the house. He knew that something wasn't right. We never really talked about it because we don't teach kids what to say in those situations. It would simply hover between us, but although we didn't discuss the abuse, Mark made me feel like a normal kid. For a while, at least.

Still, we couldn't do all of childhood's "normal" activities. For example, he never spent the night at the house. I would never ask him because my mom was so emotionally abusive, and who was around didn't matter. She would yell and scream at me or whoever was in her orbit, and I didn't want to subject him to that. It was too embarrassing for both of us.

I was allowed to stay with him a couple of times, which was very odd. My mother constantly tried to keep me at home, so I wouldn't share many things that were going on. However, because his house was only four houses down, I think the proximity made her feel at least somewhat in control.

One of those times made me realize how abnormal my home life was. For the longest time, I thought all parents hit their children or yelled at them. I thought it was standard. Then, one night, Mark invited me to his house for dinner.

When I stepped inside, it was like entering the Land of Oz. His house was clean and tidy. He had two parents, Roger and Mary, who were warm and affectionate with each other. While Mary cooked, Roger would come up behind her and kiss her neck.

"Mom," said Mark. We stood in the kitchen while his twin brothers chased each other with foam swords. "This is Chad."

She turned and smiled at me warmly. "It's very nice to meet you, Chad."

I couldn't take my eyes off how bright and clean everything was—no dirty dishes in the sink. The floors were polished. The whole energy of the room was fun and relaxed, not tense and angry, as it was at my house. Then, I remembered what Margaret had taught me. I always wanted to make her proud. "Thank you," I replied.

"Can I take your sweater?" she asked.

Obediently, I pulled it over my head. My hair became ruffled in the process. Mary, seeing the disarray, laughed and said, "Let me fix that cowlick." She reached out her hand toward my head.

My reaction was immediate and unconscious. I flinched away from her, my heart pounding. All I had seen was a hand reach up, and in my house, that usually meant a slap would follow.

Mary's forehead wrinkled in confusion, and a wave of embarrassment swept over me, though I didn't understand why—the moment passed quickly, though, as Mark's little siblings ran in and asked me to play.

That whole evening was a series of small surprises. When it came time for dinner, everyone gathered around the table. We said grace, then passed around the food. Not once during that whole evening did Mary or Roger yell or hit their children, which I thought was very odd, but I liked it. We laughed, told stories, and Roger and Mary sometimes held hands at the table. I wondered what it was like to grow up in a house like that. I wasn't envious of Mark; simply filled with curiosity. What was it like to have two parents? Or sitting down to dinner every evening?

The longing would come later, though. When I returned to my own house, where my mother screamed at me from the moment I walked through the door, I remembered that there was another way.

A better way.

There's only so long that people can observe violence without saying something about it. For years, Bob and Margaret protected me as best as they knew how. They didn't want to see me gobbled up by the system, but with Bob's cancer diagnosis, they knew he didn't have long to live. I think that finally made them pull the trigger into telling Child Protective Services; they knew they wouldn't be around to protect me, so someone needed to.

One day, someone knocked on the door when I was at their house. I had all my toys spread out on the floor, and I was playing with them like I usually did after school.

Margaret tried to warn me that there would be a visitor. "Chad, there's a very nice lady coming over, and she's just going to talk to us. You don't have to do anything special, just play like normal."

That's weird, I thought. You don't tell someone to act normal if there's nothing to worry about. Still, I didn't think much of Margaret's words until she arrived.

When the woman in the suit entered the living room, I instantly knew something was up. She had short blond hair, and she wore dark pants. She carried a small, handheld camera and a notebook in a blue, leather case.

"Hi," she greeted me. Even though she smiled, she had an air of fatigue about her, like she had seen too much. "My name is Connie."

I glanced at Margaret. "It's good to meet you, Connie."

Margaret smiled at me; I had practiced my good manners.

"I'm just going to talk with Bob and Margaret some, OK?"

I got scared because I knew she was an authority figure, so I started picking up my toys and putting them away. I wanted to "be on my best behavior," as Bob and Margaret always told me. Would she take me away from Bob and Margaret if I didn't act right? Why was she there? What if I made a mistake?

"No, just play like normal," Margaret insisted. "Don't worry about anything."

"Yeah, just pretend like I'm not even here."

I didn't quite believe her, but I tried to play anyway. I found out later that she was there to observe me playing in various environments: Bob and Margaret's house, school, and my own home.

When they showed up at my school to take pictures, everyone stared. This time, though, I didn't mind. Some part of me knew that Connie cared about me, that someone might remove me from my mother's house. Then, right in the middle of class, the CPS worker walked in, took pictures of my bruises, and made notes while I studied. Once again, I was the weird kid, but all I could think was, "My life is about to be saved. I'm going to be saved."

It was like seeing the light in a dark forest or when you flip on a switch, and roaches start scattering. For once, I had hope that things would finally get better.

Someone is going to get me out of here, I thought. Maybe I can live with Bob and Margaret forever.

The only problem with roaches is that they can move fast.

My bedroom door flies open. My mother smiles while holding the doorknob. "Yes, I'll leave it up to you." She bends down, just inches from my face. Her breath reeks like dirty feet; her brown eyes are cold and filled with disgust. I wish I could turn away; I wish I was back in our basement alone. Then, in a slow, croaky voice, she says, "If you think I treat you so damn bad, Chad, you can leave!"

For a second, I snapped out of my defensive style and took a chance by looking at the front door. My mind begins to drift. I don't understand the new game she is playing with me. All of a sudden, I realize that this is no game. It takes thirty seconds or so for me to understand this is my chance, my shot.

By this time, I had wanted to run away for years, but some indivisible fear within kept me from doing it. I told myself, this is too easy. I so badly wanted to move my thin legs beneath me, but they remained still. "Well, Chad?" Mother screams in my ear. "It's your choice!" Time at this moment seems to stand still as my eyes focus on the shag carpet in our living room. "You don't have the guts to leave your mother, little boy. Knock it off!"

I can feel my little body shake. I close my eyes tightly for a moment, wishing myself away into nothing. In my mind, I can see myself walking through the door. I smile inside, giving me a small amount of courage from the goosebumps running down my back. I so badly wanted to leave.

The more I envisioned myself walking through the front door, the more I began to feel the warmth spread through my soul. I can feel my body moving. My brown eyes pop open. I look down at my worn-out sneakers; my feet are stepping through the front door. Oh my God, what the hell am I doing? Out of fear of my mother, I dare not stop.

"There, you did it, buddy boy," Mother victoriously states. "I didn't force you to do anything!" I stepped through our front door, knowing full damn well that Mother would reach out and yank me back into the house. I can still feel the hairs on my neck standing up. After stepping past the door, I quicken my pace. I turn left and walk down the cement steps. I hear Mother's loud voice from behind me yelling, "You'll be back; you won't leave your mother!"

My chipped teeth begin to chatter. My thrill of the great escape begins to wear off. My mind starts to trick me. Maybe, Mother was right. As much as she beat and yelled at me, my room was warmer than out here. Besides, I tell myself I do lie and steal. So maybe I do deserve to be punished like this. I stop for a second to rethink my plan. If I turn back now, right now, she'll yell and beat the hell out of me. But I am used to that. If I'm lucky enough, I'll be back in bed by the night's end. A few short hours later, a police officer approached me outside the donut shop and asked me my name and how old I was. Soon I found myself in the front seat of the police car headed back to my mother. I arrived home just in time to see my mother leaving for work. The evil grin on her face told me that I was in grave danger.

My mother grabbed my little arm. I jerked from the force and struck my head against the top of the car. "For Christ's sake Chad, can't you just stay out of trouble and out of the way? Can you do that?" Mother yells, raising her voice so loud I can feel my skin crawl. Slowly, I nod yes while looking down as I walk back into the house.

The insults and punishment continued as soon as we got in. Soon, the day becomes night; my only fear is my mother and what she'll do to me next.

Best Friends

Back in the early 80s, I only had two friends I considered real friends. They were both neighbors that just lived down the street. *Mark Bond* was probably my best friend my entire life, even until now. *Matt* lived a couple of blocks away. We would hang out a lot in elementary school. I would bring my jam box and have a big group follow us around the recess area. Mark just lived about five houses away, so we spent quite a bit of time together. Our favorite thing back then was to play wiffle ball in his backyard or my front yard. I remember what our bases consisted of back then. First base was a water meter. Our second base was a giant oak tree, and our third base in my front yard was a bush. Then we had a plastic home plate that was used in the garden of Margaret and Bob's house. And in the Indiana winter, we would shovel the snow to play. Or we would go to the basketball court and shovel the snow off to play during the bitter Indiana cold. Matt and I connected on a different level. Music was our thing. We'd watch MTV and play in our jam boxes with cassette tapes outside his house. I was constrained with my time with Matt and Mark because of my mother's abuse and restrictions on what I could do outside.

I always believed there was some paranoia with my mother that wouldn't allow me to go outside and have traditional friends since she'd be afraid I'd just go outside and run off. So, when the opportunity presented itself, I would always watch cartoons at Mark's house. I was captivated by cartoons like Tom and Jerry, the Flintstones, Scooby-Doo, and Bugs Bunny. However, at home, I retreated and retreated further inside of myself in silence.

While the beatings continued, life moved forward. It was 1983, and I had just turned ten years old. The big hair bands of 1983 began to change. While 1983 followed many of the trends, there were some notable events. In the world of music, David Bowe hit the number 1 chart with his single, Let's Dance. On the big screen at the movie theaters, Star Wars Return of the Jedi was still taking over box sales tickets. Scarface and A Christmas Story tied for 2nd with the highest ticket sales in 1983. The president then was Ronald

Reagan. He was the 40th president of the United States. On June 6th of that year, Betty White became the first woman to win outstanding woman host at the Daytime Emmy Awards. That year, my Chicago Cubs went 71-91 and finished dead last in the National League East. However, in the same year, I would be able to meet my favorite baseball player, Ryan Sandler, at Wrigley Field. While my mother was out of town, I could stay at my friend's, and his parents had season tickets so I could watch at Wrigley Field. That year, the Baltimore Oilers won the word series with 98 wins. As we left the ballpark, I had a rare sense of happiness.

When my SAT scores came back from school, a simple but confused principal was forced to make what I'm sure was a difficult decision. My scores were so low he was in disbelief at how I ever made it to the fourth grade. I tested on a second-grade level in nearly every subject other than one. In addition, the report read, I suffer from significant headaches because my mother had slapped me, hit me, shoved me in the head every day since my dad had walked out of our lives.

My highest score on the SATs, with no surprise to me, was protective instincts. And again, I watched my friends move on to the next grade level, as I remained in the fourth grade for the second time. I had failed the first grade, the second grade, and now the fourth grade. I would be lucky if I were to live to see the fifth grade. Because I failed so much, I was much taller than the other students. I couldn't run or catch and would stutter if anyone I thought was important would talk to me. I barely knew any of my timetables. And the subject they called History was a word they used to describe me when I got older, they would say. Others would laugh, teachers would pass me up when reading out loud, and a handful of older students would bully me at the first chance they had.

I reached the fifth grade, and one encounter in a hallway would lead me to learn an unlikely sport. After the worst time in school, I finally reached the fifth grade. My teacher had heard about me and what I lacked and took the continence of the emotional abuse upon herself, whereas my mother forgot Mrs. H would not. Her words were fierce, angry, and hurtful. I lacked reading knowledge and was on display for her to be the class joke. The joke was, "Class, this is what happens when you don't come to school because you're lazy." I would look at the floor, not wanting anyone to know my pain.

One of those unlikely meetings would change my way of thinking. That afternoon, I would meet Mr. Joe Moore, and my young life would never be the same. On an April day after school, I approached the water cooler in the hallway adjacent to the gym. The gym door swings open, and a basketball rolls into the hallway against the cooler. I bend over to pick it up, and Coach Moore yells, "Get back in here!"

I stood there holding that ball, not knowing what the hell was happening. Again, he says, "Get back in here!" I stuttered, "I don't play basketball, I could never make the team like those guys." He replied, "Don't ever let someone's opinion of you stop you from your dreams Mr. Gaines!" For the first time in my life, someone believed in me and called me Mr. Gaines. I felt alive, but Basketball, I thought? The first drill was dribbling a basketball while wearing blinders.

The meaning of blinders was so you would not be able to see the ball but feel it. The team was amazed that Coach Moore had me do it with two balls simultaneously. I had a natural feeling because I always had to react before my next beating at home before I could see it coming. The more Coach Moore would push, the more I would lead. The deal was, to stay on the team, and the school would agree to let my mother know I was staying after school to do makeup homework. I was now starting to gain some ground in my life.

Momentum Fades

A man sits across the table from me in *North Beach* and asks, "Tell me about your life Chad." I nod my head and smile at him. I think back to what now seems to be a lifetime ago in a dark place in Northern Indiana. I look out the window toward Grant Street and begin to share my life. My life? It's not the easiest thing to explain or to talk about. It has not been the dreamy, fabulous, or famous life I considered it would be. It's had more ups and downs than the city streets here in San Francisco. All I wanted to do as a young boy; my only dream was: to live long enough to go to places they said I couldn't go due to my circumstances. I've been blessed to *accomplish* that here.

The romantics of San Francisco would call my life a love story or a tale about someone that never gave up. However, the non-believers and my critics would dismiss it as a mess and a tragedy of a wasted life. The truth is, my friend, it's a little of both. No matter how I view it after hearing this today, I have no complaints about my path and the places it has taken me. I wouldn't have had it any other way. Unfortunately, it's still not easy to share what I'm about to share. Nevertheless, it's about a promise I made to a little boy so many years ago.

I first came to San Francisco three years ago on a Greyhound bus with seven dollars, a backpack of clothes, and a dream of walking across the Golden Gate. What I've discovered about my forty years of life is that Love always finds its way home no matter where home is. I remember those moments when I didn't think I would make it. The blistering glare of the California sun from the Beach St. sign blinds me as I open my eyes to start my day. I sit up, brush myself off, and look toward the beautiful California sky.

I carry my black backpack, which contains my remaining clothes, a toothbrush, a notebook, and a razor to shave so no one will know I am homeless. I'm just the piece of the man I used to be a few years ago. I'm so far away from home now. Where is home anyway? I have slept outside on these steps for nearly ten months while working full-time and training most of the staff. It has been an unbearable journey from where I was to where I am. Yet, I get the motivation that keeps me alive because I won't give up on my dreams.

Throughout those cold nights, my body often shakes because of the San Francisco winds and cold. I lost over thirty pounds in the last few months, and my hair is starting to fall out. I'm being pulled apart from the inside out with something controlling my body and emotional state, yet I press on for my dreams and a promise.

The American Encyclopedia describes home as; a dwelling place used as a permanent or semi-permanent residence for an individual, family, household, or several families in a tribe. Those good old days of home, family, fun, and friends are mostly gone from my life. "Explain to me what you're trying to imply, Chad," he said. "Well, it's kind of funny and sad at the same time."

I had no clue what I was getting into that night. I got on the Greyhound bus to come to San Francisco and the experiences that I would go through. I guess in the same way, we all had a dream once. I think as a little boy, all I wanted to do was to live. I always had a bigger picture of the world and the opportunity it could give us if we kept pushing. I discovered that around the age of five, I think. Those moments when you're too young to understand but just old enough to know something is wrong.

I think you remember those early days I talked about. He replied, "I do, but I'm still a little baffled to what you mean with your own life." I have to go back to help you understand what I mean and who I am today. I have to take you back with me to a place and time when things in life were different, much different. It's a very dark place I don't usually talk about. In my life, I have seen, discovered, found, lost, and rediscovered things that can only be described by doctors, friends, co-workers, and business professionals worldwide as "the hand of God has been on you."

For I reckon that the sufferings of this present time are not worthy to be compared with the glory which shall be revealed in us.

Romans 8:18

Full of Pride

Smack! Smack! Mother smacks me in the face, and I fall to the floor. I know better by this time in my young life to look her in the eyes. She takes that as an act of defiance. Another blow from her pushes my head toward the kitchen counter. I let my tears pour as a sign of my defeat. She changes her mind by the second by turning and simply walking out of the kitchen. She enjoys using her force as a weapon against me. I never have the strength to crawl away, even if it means saving my life.

Mother had never acted this bizarre in some time. I knew something was clearly wrong, and I would pay for it. For months now, I had found some peace in our damp basement. I use the basement to plan what might be Mother's next move. Mother likes that I am in the basement and out of her way. The windows are screwed shut in case I was to escape from the basement.

She also ensures that the windows are covered with aluminum foil so I cannot view the outside. What first started as a place to escape Mother's rage has now become my dungeon.

I can hear Mother walking back and forth through the kitchen, talking on the phone and complaining about some of her belongings missing again—my white record player blasts Michael Jackson's "Thriller" album. I dance whenever I hear "Beat It" on my record. I use the album as my strength against Mother's blows. The music puts me in another place. I drift far away from our little town. I nod my head from side to side and moonwalk through parts of the damp basement.

Suddenly, the basement door crashes open at the top of the stairway. Mother's shadow enters my sight. Her hands appear to be placed on her hips as she looks fiercely down the steps toward where I was dancing for a few moments.

"Chad Richard, turn that dumb shit off!"

I stumbled as I rushed to shut off my record player. I run inside of myself somewhere, *knowing* what will come next. The old wooden steps start to creak from Mother's weight. Mother stops midway down the steps and bends down to get me in eyesight.

With a hand motion, Mother directs me to come where she stands. Without a sound, I take my first step, then another toward the basement stairs, where Mother stands with an evil grimace. Her dirty shade of hair appears as if she had caught her finger in a light socket and glimmers in the basement light.

Mother starts to rage about my *"N"* music that I constantly blasted while playing in the basement. Then, out of the blue, Mother punches me with the force of a locomotive in my nose. I lose the fight to keep my balance on the steps and begin to tumble back down the wooden steps.

Over and over, I plunge back down the hard steps. Finally, I come to rest in a pile of dirty clothes. Mother shouts, *"While you're down there, start a load of clothes!"* She slams the door on her way back up the stairs to the kitchen.

I lay dazed, trying to figure out what just happened. "It came so fast," I said to myself. I try to stand to my feet as I wipe the blood off my face. My knees are weak and wobbly, and I fall once again to the floor. The blood is pouring into my mouth from my nose.

I hear Mother stirring around the kitchen. I try but fail to hold back my tears from the blows Mother had unleashed on my body. I feel my head spin out of control. I use a dirty shirt to press against my bloody nose. My nose is throbbing to the point I am about to pass out. Several minutes passed before I came to and realized what happened. Blood still runs from a massive wound on the top of my nose.

At first, I thought it was just a bloody nose. However, it is far worse than it first appeared. The blood won't stop pouring as I fall back into bewilderment again and go unconscious. Everything goes black. My lifeless little body is positioned next to the pile of dirty clothes. Seconds are passing. I try to wobble back to my feet with one sneaker on and the other lost amidst my plunge off the many stairs. After the second time of coming, I *stumble* to my feet. I look up at the closed basement door and clench my fist in victory.

"Yes she is gone!" I cried.

Early the next morning, as I tried to step out of bed, I discovered that I could barely bend my legs. I enter the bathroom, look into the mirror and smile, and she can't kill me. Some say we are being taught lessons every day of our life.

You know, since that night in our basement, I had the overwhelming feeling that maybe God wanted me to meet a few *wrong* people before meeting the *right* one. Eventually, I would find the right people in a most unlikely place.

The Fight for Survival

One night after dinner, Mother called out, "Let's check that damn room of yours, and your mother will decide if you can go outside!" My old wooden bedroom door slowly opens. I felt my world shake like one of those California earthquakes. I sat at our kitchen table, waiting for the verdict. Minutes pass in silence. I couldn't tell at that moment what was more frightening, my mother's rage or her silence. Finally, Mother shouted, "Oh Mr. Chad, come here, little boy!"

I *still sit* there at the table, eating as much food as my little body could hold before her next out-of-control action. I managed to slide my legs out from underneath the table and stand on my feet. I slowly walked down the hallway leading to my bedroom door. I slowly pushed the door open, fearing what would be next. I entered my *bedroom* with my head looking down at the wooden floor. Looking at her was a sign of disrespect to her authority. Mother started yelling in my face before knocking me upside the head. The blood ran from my mouth as backhands continued to come.

Her hands reach out for my hair. With a stronghold, she whips me to my bed, then turns and slams the bedroom door on her way out. I lay there bewildered and completely covered in blood from the blows to my mouth. Something inside of me wouldn't let me give up. A few minutes later, I hear her ramble something down the hall. I'm not too confident about what she says. However, fearful she will finish where she started on me.

Better a patient person than a warrior, one with self-control than one who takes a city. -Proverbs 16:32

My life would soon be turned *upside down*. Toward the end of 1983, my caregiver Margaret died of her long struggle with cancer. A year later her husband Bob would soon follow by dying less than a year later. The days that followed his memorial service were hard to understand for an 11-year-old boy. My safety net, which Margaret and Bob once gave me, was now gone forever. A part of me died that day.

Left (is me at age 4) Right. (My dad Richard) 1977

My only solace was knowing they left me something in their will. I knew their house belonged to me; they had explained it enough times before they died. In my mind, I thought that maybe I could live in the house by myself. Since my mother never cared for me, I thought I could survive on my own. Things like water and electricity bills didn't cross my mind; in my head, I built up this picture of making peanut butter sandwiches and doing my homework in peace. I reasoned that if things got terrible, I could stay with Mark and his family for a while.

Of course, that wasn't what happened.

As soon as Bob died, my mother went to my grandmother with the will.

"Look at this," she said, waving the papers before her face. My mother had this look of maniacal glee in her eyes.

My grandmother lowered her reading glasses, and her small, piggy eyes skimmed over the legal jargon. The only thing she picked up was "will" and "Chad." "They left it to *him*?" She said the word, like you might say, "garbage." "He's just a boy."

"They left everything to him. The house. The cars. They even have a tractor."

My grandmother's eyes widened. "Oh reeeeally..." The word was pulled out like taffy. She looked at me like she was considering squashing me under her heel. "We'll get a lawyer. He's just a minor. He can't be expected to own the house."

"Aren't lawyers expensive?" my mother asked.

"Don't be stupid," replied my grandmother. "This is a house we're talking about. And it's paid off." She flipped through the pages. "*And* they have money in a savings account?" She raised her glasses, and they perched on top of her head. "I know someone. We'll break the will. Get all the rights transferred to us."

And that's precisely what they did. At the time, Bob and Margaret didn't set up an estate to protect the money until I was eighteen. I'm not sure if they understood how to or simply trusted in the goodwill of my family.

So they contested the will and took everything. It was a fairly easy decision for the courts; they didn't know a CPS investigation was ongoing, and on the surface, it was pretty obvious what should happen. All they saw was that an eleven-year-old kid had suddenly been willed an entire house, $200K in savings, and cars. They appointed my mother and grandmother guardians, but they just had a big estate sale.

I had to watch as they sold everything from Bob and Margaret's house: furniture, plates, and cutlery, my television from the basement, and my model trains. They even sold my clothes and toys.

In a way, that felt like losing Bob and Margaret all over again. First, I had to deal with their death, but I had thought that I would still be able to live in their house. Now it was gone. My refuge from the world, gone. All connection to them, simply gone.

Lakeland, Florida

When my bus pulled up in front of my house, I knew something was wrong. A U-Haul truck was parked in the driveway. For one brief moment, I thought that maybe my mother was moving away, and I would have to live with Bob and Margaret. My mother shattered that illusion when I walked inside.

Half-taped boxes and moving supplies were everywhere. Silverware clanked in the kitchen as my mother threw everything haphazardly into boxes without wrapping much or labeling anything.

"What's going on?" I asked.

She looked up at me. "We're leaving. Grab your shit and put it in the truck."

"But why—"

"Just do it!" She glanced at the clock on the wall. "Now!"

I ran to my bedroom, panic squeezing my chest. Why was there a truck? Where were we going? Would we come back?

I thought that maybe we were just going out of town on vacation. Spring break was close, and every other kid in class talked about how they would leave town to visit family. I had no idea I was about to leave my town of 500 people for a city of more than 100,000.

Thinking that we would return, I took some clothes, my favorite toys, and a few other things that were dear to me. I filled up my backpack. I didn't have much time. Soon, my mother stuck her head in the door.

"Time to go."

Then we left.

As Mother and I drove the 2,000 miles to the middle of sunny Florida, what I didn't know as a little boy was, why we were moving far away from our home in little town Indiana. The truth would be foretold during my *teen years* why the fast move that led us thousands of miles away from home. During the years from 1982-1984, the local child protective services began an independent investigation for child abuse in my home. Once that was made clear to my mother, we made a *run for it* one afternoon after school. I arrived home that day to find a huge, orange Ryder truck parked against our front door.

I was nearly 13 years old when our moving truck, driven by my mother, pulled into the *sunshine state* of Florida. The more my mother yelled, the more she spat on me when she was frustrated, and the more I kept telling myself, *"One Day I Will"* do great things so no one has to suffer what I'm going through now. I kept telling myself over and over and over again that one day I would make a difference in this world. Even then, I believed I would.

...*Two Years Later*...

I knew something was wrong when all my clothes were on the driveway. All my belongings were scattered: my school books, clothes, and what few toys I had. We had been in Florida for two years, and I was now fifteen years old when I was thrown out of the house.

I walked up to the door, but it was locked. I grabbed the handle and twisted it, but the door wouldn't budge. I banged with my fist. "It's me!" I shouted through the door. "Open the door." I looked around. I lived in a poor neighborhood, and I had to watch out. Making noise could mean trouble, and I quickly learned that it was best to keep your head down.

My mother didn't open the door, but she shouted so I could hear: "You're big enough for yourself. You figure it out."

My jaw dropped. What was I supposed to do now? Where was I supposed to go?

Anger boiled inside me. It had been rough transitioning from a tiny town to a sprawling metropolis. From the moment I arrived in Florida, I felt tiny. Now the one lifeline I had—staying in a house, however awful it was—was cut off from me.

I turned around in shock. At first, I couldn't believe it. My mother was throwing me out of the house? The wind tossed my clothes around, and I chased after them. I could only do the next thing that came to mind. That is how I learned to survive. I didn't know where I would go or what I would eat, or where I would sleep. All I could do was bend down and gather what little I could carry. After picking up and dusting off my clothes, I wandered the town.

I was so angry at my mother that I wandered for a long time. My thoughts buzzed around my head, and I raged at the injustice of it. Even though I knew that minors couldn't be left alone, I didn't want to go to CPS because my life had taken a turn for the worse the last time they had gotten involved. With each step, my anger seemed to cement into something hard in my chest. Of everything I had endured from my mother, this seemed one of the most cruel— complete and utter abandonment—the ultimate rejection.

What did I do to deserve this?

Was I so horrible, so unwanted that a mother would throw out her son? I kept thinking of everything I could have done to prevent it. Should I have been nicer to her? Play by her rules more? I started to believe that I wasn't worth love or affection if my mother didn't want me to live with her.

Eventually, I made my way to a softball field. I found an unlocked part of the fence, so I slipped inside one of the dugouts. Thankfully, Florida has warm nights, so I put on a few layers of clothing, laid on the hard bench, closed my eyes, and fell asleep.

NEW CHAPTER

Rows and rows of canned beans filled my vision. I reached into a carton, filled my arms with more cans, and carefully placed them on the shelves. I was bored to tears, and the broken speaker in the store shouted a staticky, barely comprehensible noise above me. I wanted to take a baseball bat and smash it to bits.

Because I didn't have anywhere to stay and suddenly no reliable pantry to get food from, I dropped out of school and found a job at a grocery store. I was only fifteen, but the owners believed me when I said I was sixteen and didn't ask too many questions about why I wasn't in school.

A bell clanged that announced someone was walking in. I didn't pay much attention until my friend Rex approached me. I had met Rex in school; like me, he had dropped out too. And, like me, he was used to hard living; he stayed with me sometimes in the softball field dugout when he wasn't staying with whatever girlfriend he had at the time.

"Hey wassup, man," said Rex.

"Shit." I gestured to the cans of beans. "Nothing much."

Rex hit me in the chest with the back of his hand. "How much you make here?"

"Twenty-seven bucks."

The minimum wage at the time was about $3.35, and I had a standard 8-hour shift.

Rex laughed and leaned in. "You wanna make two hundred for an hour's work?"

My eyebrows rose to the ceiling. "Doing what?"

He grinned and said, "C'mon, I'll show you."

I yanked off my store apron and left that second. Rex and I took a bus to an electronics store halfway across town. We sat across a homeless guy who mumbled to himself, and Rex explained the plan.

"It's real easy. You talk to the security guard. Distract him. Don't make a big fuss or nothing, just keep him occupied. While you do that, I'm going to take one of their stereos. Not the high grades ones, but not the shitty ones, either."

I was nervous. I had never stolen anything before and didn't know what to expect.

However, it was, as Rex said, surprisingly simple. I talked to the security guard, and Rex walked out of the store with a stereo when no one was looking. The shop didn't have metal detectors, and it was small enough that they didn't have an extensive security staff.

We then took it to a pawn shop, where we sold it.

When that money hit my hand, I was hooked. It was much easier than working eight hours a day in a boring grocery store, where customers looked down on me and drove me nuts with their neediness.

Over time, we shared the responsibility for the theft. I would be the one to lift whatever our target was, and I eventually gained the respect and admiration of Rex's friends that way.

So my downward spiral began with hanging around the wrong crowd, and I did so because they were the only ones around me at the time. I wasn't in school, and I had to find whatever help I could. So much guilt, bitterness, and anger from my childhood built up like a storm inside me that I was willing to do things just to be a part of a group. However, my group of "friends" was part of a gang I wanted to join. However, that group would be a gang leading to my arrest fifteen years later.

The thing was that they made it feel like a family unit. I never had any siblings or father; this was a new family I found. We watched out for each other and took on each other's quarrels. If someone insulted or messed with one person's close friend or family, it was like insulting the entire group. The more time I spent with them, the more I wanted to be a part of it, but I also played the part. I was angry, ready to pick a fight with the whole world.

Entering the gang wasn't easy, though. First, I had to prove my loyalty and my desire to be a part of the gang. I also had to prove that I was trustworthy. The leaders knew about my petty thefts from Rex, so they gave me new challenges. They told me, "If you want to run with us, this is what you have to do."

So I did a lot of petty thefts initially, like stealing radios or other electronics, but I soon graduated to more significant crimes. My "test" to enter the gang was stealing a car. Once I did that, I was initiated.

Plus, it became a way to support my drug habit.

I can't explain why or the date when I first started using alcohol and experimenting with drugs. I think it was around the time I turned fourteen. It began at a friend's house in his dad's liquor cabinet as fun for me. What I thought was funny, my friend saw it as an everyday routine to take away the embarrassment of getting sexually abused by his dad. For me, I have never seen alcohol in that way. However, the first time I experimented with drugs was far different.

Very early in my teenage life, I discovered that drugs were my cover for all my hurt and feelings of abandonment, lack of education, and abuse.

At first, I sold drugs. Once I was initiated into the gang, I had some level of street cred and street smarts. I could approach a dealer and offer to sell his supply. He would give me a portion and tell me how much cash I needed to bring back and what my take-home fee was. I made $1,000 per day.

But I soon went from making a grand per day to using a grand per day. I also did several flat-out stupid things that would nearly get me killed. But I'll get to that in a moment.

The first drug I was introduced to at a city park after football practice was cocaine. A friend and a football player from my team gave a little bit to me to "help me run faster." It instantly hit my bloodstream and made me feel like the Terminator. I ran faster, moved faster, blocked harder, and the feeling from cocaine lasted for many hours.

I started using it every Tuesday and Thursday at football practice. I was able to push harder than most. In the beginning, my $200 drug habit grew to over a thousand dollars a week in just months. I wasn't sleeping; I wasn't going to school. And when I was going to school, I couldn't focus on my studies, nor did I care to. On our football team in 1986, we only had twelve players. That meant eleven players played offense and defense the entire game and every play. Most of us were exhausted. The majority of us were either drunk or high on cocaine just to keep up with teams that were bigger, faster, and stronger. Most of my teammates, including me, came from dangerous parts of the city. For us, city league football was our only way out. Our grades were too poor to play for the school.

So with a small fee, a parent signature, in most cases, the coach himself would sign for us, you were suiting up for the Lakeland Patriots city league football team on Saturday mornings. I learned quickly that the anger and violence I had inherited from my parents through their behavior would soon be my undoing.

I was right in the middle of it all, the drugs, the liquor, the shootings, the gangs, and the parties. By the time I turned fourteen in June, I was introduced to heroin for the first time as a birthday gift from a gang member at our Junior high. Heroin took me to another place in my life as a teenager. It had a different feeling altogether as if you were falling out of an airplane. It took all the pain of the past away. It put me in a different state of mind. It simply did the opposite of what cocaine did. Cocaine was my rush, and heroin was my instant downer, like floating on a cloud.

I soon dropped out of high school and began my life on the streets as a gang member and drug dealer to support my habit. Two of the top players on our 1988 team went on to play at the University of Florida State and the University of Miami. Lakeland, Florida, a city of nearly 130,000, is also known as the longtime spring training base for the Detroit Tigers baseball team and is also named for its 38 lakes.

Lakeland is a larger city in Polk County, Florida, just 35 minutes from Tampa. Things in the world were changing. At that time, the world was moving, moving fast. Change was the word that people used. The culture became hard rock music nearly overnight, it seemed. The music television channel, or MTV, streamed on television sets worldwide, and President Ronald Reagan was the current President of the United States.

On the 12th day in June of 1987, President Reagan and his speech at the Berlin Wall awestruck most of America.

"We welcome change and openness; for we believe that freedom and security go together, that the advance of human liberty can only strengthen the cause of world peace. There is one sign the Soviets can make that would be unmistakable, that would advance dramatically the cause of freedom and peace. General Secretary Gorbachev, if you seek peace, if you seek prosperity for the Soviet Union and eastern Europe, if you seek liberalization, come here to this gate. Mr. Gorbachev, open this gate. Mr. Gorbachev, tear down this wall!" Just two years later, "that wall" in Berlin would in fact come down.

An incredible moment in history; however, far from the Berlin Wall in East Germany, I was buying and selling drugs nearly day and night in Lakeland, Florida. I learned about life on the streets very quickly. I was almost fifteen, lost, and high everywhere I went. When my mother kicked me to the streets, I never looked back. The gang and drugs were my family now. I remember standing in the hallway in our junior high school, and a basketball coach once asked me, "Chad, you have incredible talent, yet you never use it. Do you care if you live or die?" I stood there in shock. No one in my entire life has asked me that before. He looked at me in the eyes and said, "That's what I thought, that's what I thought."

I had few friends that I could skip school with and get high, more enemies than anything, however. I was cheating death one day at a time. The first incredibly dumb thing I did was sell drugs from one gang to another. I was the white kid, the middle man, so to speak, in the operations to keep the peace, yet not let anyone know what I was doing. When the money began to come up short, or the cocaine weighed less than the average, I was the number one target.

They would drive by my mother's house and throw bricks at her windows, spray gang graffiti on her car, and threaten to kill me daily through the phone. I wore red on one side of the city and near my old house, I wore blue. One evening I arrived at football practice and had a blue rag hanging out of my pocket as I dressed in my football pads. At the time, I didn't know that one of our other players was a relative of the other side's gang. It wouldn't be long before they would connect the two and discover what I was doing between two rival gangs. That same weekend after our Saturday football game, my life would change.

The other incredibly dumb thing that I did was steal the drugs entirely. A dealer would give me his supply, and I promised to bring back the money, but I disappeared. I stole $10,000 worth of drugs and used it all in a matter of days. I never thought I would get caught. Lakeland was such a big city that I never thought I would reencounter the drug dealer.

It was an assumption that I would come to regret. I would get shot in the head and live to tell about it, but I didn't know. The only thing on my mind was winning a football game.

At halftime, we were leading 13-10 against Bartow on our home field. I followed my teammates off the field toward the 50-yard line that led to our locker room.

A man out of the crowd yelled, *"Good job Chad,* good job!" The tall, thin white man didn't fit in here, yet he looked like I'd seen him before. I stopped to wave and continued to head into the locker room. I didn't think much of him and put him out of my head quickly after showering and changing. After a heartbreaking loss to Bartow, which was a much bigger and stronger team than ours, I would soon be sitting face to face with a man that, 20 years earlier, I called dad. As fast as my dad walked out of my life, somewhere in the hot summer of the middle of a Florida city, he would reenter my life briefly.

I left the locker room, and the unfamiliar man grabbed my arm. "Chad," he said. "It's me. It's your dad."

Shock mixed with rage as I recognized him. I was so surprised that I could barely speak. Here he was, the man who walked out of my life, in the flesh, right before my eyes. Yet, instead of feeling happy, I was so angry.

How dare you walk back into my life as if you didn't abandon me? I thought.

I jerked my arm away. "What do you want?" I demanded.

He seemed surprised at my harsh tone like he had expected a warmer welcome. "Well, I'm in town for a few days, and I tracked you down. I was wondering if you'd like to get something to eat."

"What, you mean right now?"

He shrugged. "Sure."

He drove us to a nearby restaurant. The car ride was one of the most awkward moments I had experienced. We didn't talk much; we just let the radio play in the background. I was still feeling horrible about our team's loss, mad at myself for not playing better, mad at our team, and embarrassed from the loss.

"You sure played well today," he offered.

My throat ached, and I swallowed. "Thanks." I made it sound as sarcastic as possible.

We pulled into a cheap diner, and I fidgeted with my drinking straw in my water as the waitress took our orders. I was so on edge around my father that I wasn't really hungry.

He lit a cigarette. "So…what have you been up to?"

Drinking. Doing drugs. Stealing drugs. Dropping out of school. Living on the street. Putting up with my mother's shit while you were having the time of your life, I thought bitterly.

"Nothing much," I replied.

The cigarette smoke smelled stale, and I hated it. I coughed.

The waitress brought our food, and my dad thanked her. He lifted up his hamburger and took a bite. "Staying out of trouble?"

I picked up a French fry and stabbed it into the ketchup. "Sure."

I wanted to yell, *"Where have you been? Where were you when my dam life was falling apart? What kind of fun were you having while Mother was nearly beating me to death, you son of a bitch?"*

I briefly imagined spitting on him, like my mother used to do to me. I imagined how good it would feel to just punch him in the face like my mother used to do to me, but I didn't. I didn't do anything. It took all my willpower to sit there, eating, but I told myself that even if I beat him up, that wouldn't turn back the clock. I sat across the table with this strange man that was my dad while he smoked his last cigarette.

I wanted to ask him so many questions: *why did you leave? Was I not worth it? Why did you stay away for so long? Why did you decide to come back now?*

But, I knew at the moment at that restaurant table that my life now had nothing to do with him other than the anger I carried.

I stood up. "You think you can just waltz into my life and buy me a greasy burger and everything is ok between us? Huh?" I threw my napkin on the table, my half-eaten burger sitting there, gathering flies. I pointed at him. "Fuck you." I walked out and left.

Falling Behind

All that anger needed an outlet. I released it in violent and destructive ways, which fueled my being part of a gang. It also led to a cycle of getting arrested, out on bond, and re-arrested. When I was arrested for gang activity, I had 15 pending charges.

One of those came from an incident that stemmed from protecting my cousin. As I said, when someone messed with one person's family, they could incur the wrath of the entire gang.

One such person was a guy from another town who was causing a lot of trouble with my cousin, who was about 16. By this time, I had been a part of the gang for several years. I was now a leader, people looked up to me and did what I said, and I had name recognition. So when I went into another town or city, my name carried a certain amount of weight--not a lot, but some nonetheless.

So when my cousin called me one day and said, "Chad, this guy won't leave me alone," I paid attention.

How dare he harass my little cousin? I thought.

It was like a switch; immediately, the anger rose.

Because I had lived with one for so long, I hated bullies. I hated those who picked on smaller or weaker people or even people who didn't know how to defend themselves.

"What's his name?" I asked.

He told me, and that was it. I called the other gang members and told them what was happening.

The thing is, violence just leads to violence. I had so much rage and bitterness from childhood, but I didn't realize it. I thought the only way to survive was to prove that you could hit harder and faster. I thought I had to prove that I was tough, strong, and any insult or injury to my family was like an insult to *me*.

The other thing about violence is that it also comes with a high, like any other drug. We jumped in our cars and started tracking this guy down. It wasn't tough. We spotted him one day after he was harassing my cousin. We followed his car, and my heart pounded with excitement. I told myself I wanted to protect my cousin, but I just wanted to hit someone.

So we cut them off on a road a little outside of town. There were about three other people in the car that I drove and four others in the car behind me.

This guy had plenty of friends in his truck. They weren't complete idiots; they knew what was about to happen.

My tires screeched to a stop, and the other car also hit its brakes. We were just trying to drive them out of town. I got out, and the gravel crunched underneath my shoes. The tension in the air was so thick; I could almost taste it, bitter like ash. My muscles were coiled, ready for a fight. Even though the goal was to run them out of town, part of me wanted to smash something. Show them what happened when people messed with my family.

Every step increased my heart rate, but my face was neutral. I couldn't show any fear, any hesitation.

I walked up to the car, automatically counting people and the likelihood that anyone was carrying a gun. My mind was going haywire, alert to any minute shift that might give away sudden movement, like a hand reaching for a gun or lunging, balled into a fist.

Several of my friends trailed behind me. I approached the driver's side. The window was rolled down.

I asked for "Rick."

The guy in the passenger's seat raised his hand. He glared at me. "So what?" he demanded.

"Do you know [Cousin's Name?]?"

Of course, he did, but that wasn't the point. It was almost a ritual we had to go through. I had to identify the antagonist and "read him his crime," so to speak, and he had the chance to either own up to it or deny it. If he denied it, then that meant he was the weaker one, which of course, he couldn't do.

"Yeah, I know that motherfucker," he replied. "What you gonna do?"

"I'm going to step on your throat the next time you go near him," I said. "Don't ever approach him. Don't look at him, don't speak to him, and if you touch him, I'll make you wish you were dead."

The driver laughed and looked me up and down. All he saw was some skinny, strung-out white dude. I was scrawny from not eating well and strung out on drugs, but what he didn't see were the years of hardening I had taken.

"You ain't gonna do shit, you p--- ass bitch," he said.

One of my friends grabbed my shoulder and hissed, "Hit this guy."

In the blink of an eye, that's what I did. That's all it took.

Suddenly, hell broke loose. The car door opened, and everyone spilled out. I fought the driver, trying to get to "Rick," but my other friends got there first. The pain hurts when you're in a fight, but you push through it. You use all the pent-up anger to ignore it. So even though I took several punches, all my rage came out. I swung my fists as hard as I could.

It almost turned deadly. I didn't realize that one of my friends had a baseball bat in the other car. Rick took off running off the side of the road, and my guys chased him down. It was bloody and brutal. They beat him up so severely that his face and body were covered in blood when they were through. By the time it was over, "Rick" had to be carried away in an ambulance.

He nearly died in the hospital. Thinking about what had happened, I was sick to my stomach for a while. In my heart, I never wanted anyone I fought to die.

One of his friends identified all of us in the fight and me as the instigator. I was charged with assault with a deadly weapon with the intent to kill.

Luckily, Rick made it, but the event left me shaken. Not so much the charge but that someone had nearly died from the violence.

It was one of those warning signs that I should quit and get out of the gang, but I couldn't see a way out. I thought that was the only way to live. I didn't think that I had an alternative. But we always do. We always have a choice.

The next warning sign would be at a party, where all my past double dealings would catch up with me.

...Weeks later...

"Party night at Jay's house," said one of my friends. "You there?"

Jay's house parties were famous. Music. Girls. And all the alcohol and drugs you could put into your body were served in plastic cups and plates.

I grinned. "I am so there tonight."

After a couple of high fives, I left to grab something to eat, looking carefully around me. In gang areas, everyone had their territories. You didn't cross those lines of those territories, or it could be deadly. Gunfire and fighting in the streets were an everyday occurrence near our neighborhood.

However, since I had been double-dealing, my luck would quickly run out as those boundaries were crossed.

We rolled up to Jay's party around 7 pm as the crowd gathered outside. Four of us stepped out of his 69 Chevy SS. I was feeling great, already high and ready to party. I had on my football jersey and some shorts; I had a better chance of picking up a girl if I came dressed as a sportsman.

Two others with us were football players from our team and others at the party played ball too. Tommy, a cousin of one of our teammates, walked over to hug me as a sign of respect.

The house filled up with people as quickly as our cups did with cheap alcohol. Music blasted through speakers. Everyone was crowded in the living room, dining room, spilling out into the front yard and beyond. Cars constantly pulled in and out as people arrived.

Then, I saw him. At first, I didn't recognize the drug dealer I had scammed. But then, his face coalesced in my memory.

The chances of reencountering him were minuscule. Lakeland was so big—heck, Florida was so big—that at the time when I had taken his drugs and vanished, I thought he would never find me, that I would never see him again.

We locked eyes.

He recognized me immediately. Surprise shifted toward anger in a heartbeat.

As if in slow motion, I saw him reach toward his side. I tried to back away, but people blocked me in.

Oh shit, I thought.

He pulled out a gun.

Shots rang out at the party as I fell to the floor. People screamed as chaos broke out.

The blow was like getting punched in the face by the strongest man ever. At first, my brain didn't even register the pain. Then I finally realized it was me who was shot.

"I'm shot, I'm shot!" I yelled as blood poured out the side of my face. The pain came quickly then, but not as much as the fear.

This is it, I thought. *I'm going to die.*

People were yelling, crying, and running away from the scene. All I could do was lay on the floor as people stepped on or over me, trying to escape the shooter.

As I lay there with two shots to my face, I knew I was about to die. As darkness gathered at the corners of my eyes, I thought about my dad. I imagined him bursting through the door, somehow knowledgeable of what had happened. I imagined him tackling the gunman, picking me up, and driving me to the hospital. I don't know why I expected him to rescue me that night.

The darkness in front of my eyes grew as Tommy lowered the gun and shot me for the third time.

The bullet went through my face and passed over my tongue. To this day, I still don't have my back teeth. Not many people can say that they have been shot in the head and live to tell about it; that was only one of the miracles in my life.

After I got shot, my uncle came down from Indiana and got me out of Florida. He discovered how I was living on the streets, involved in gang activity, and deep into drugs.

So I stayed with him for a short time. I got clean. It wasn't that hard to do because my hometown was tiny. There were no hard drugs like the ones I used in small-town Indiana. No supply meant no use.

After that, my life turned around for a while. Since I was clean, I could hold down a "normal" job. That lasted for about nine years. I thought I had sorted my life out and even started a serious relationship. However, that relationship led me back to drugs and toward a spiral that would lead to prison.

To make a long story short, she cheated on me. When I discovered what she had done, I was devastated. I went through all the standard emotions of a sexual and emotional betrayal—hurt, anger, disbelief, sadness, and shock, all melding into a cycle, one after the other. But, more than that, I was completely embarrassed.

However, I had never learned how to cope with my emotions healthily, so I turned back to the only thing that would make the pain disappear (at least for a little while).

Just like that, I was back to being hooked. Nine years of sobriety gone in an instant.

When I turned back to the drugs, I found the people in my same gang, just in a different area—a different "chapter," if you will. In a way, returning to the gang was familiar and, therefore, comforting. Since we naturally turn to our families in times of crisis, I turned to the only one I had ever known. Slipping back into my old ways was only too easy.

There was one crucial difference about this particular chapter in the gang: since they were so close to Illinois, they were connected to the mob in Chicago. I quickly learned that they wanted to do more for them than steal cars and sell drugs.

They wanted us to make bombs.

So we did.

I worked at a factory with a somewhat legitimate business attached to it; however, we produced explosives. From the outside, it looked like a regular factory. Just a plain building, but the inside had the machinery to make an inferno.

Those explosives were shipped to Chicago and stored at the mob's warehouses, and that way, the mob would use them whenever needed.

That's where the big money was. Being a part of that dynamic was how I coped with the pain of losing my girlfriend and how I earned enough money for my drug habit.

It went on for a long time, but the day I delivered a couch was when my entire life changed.

Conviction

I was driving my grandmother's pickup truck to deliver a couch for a neighbor, and my cousin was riding shotgun with me. We had an extra couch that we were going to give away for free. It was a normal day—the sun was shining, it was spring, so the flowers were just starting to bloom, and the air smelled fresh and sweet. Nothing about that day caused me to worry about what came next. I didn't even notice the black Ford Bronco following us—following *me*.

When I pulled up to the house and into the driveway, I finally noticed the black Bronco. It pulled up parallel to the house, blocking me in.

Weird, I thought. It had pulled up quickly, so I felt the driver wanted to say something. The Bronco kept its engine rumbling. The car creeped me out; it was a feeling, a sense of intuition I had gained through my years of tangoing with the underworld.

Turning to my cousin, I said, "Stay here. I'll check it out."

I opened the door, placed my foot on the ground, and took three steps toward the car.

Then everything seemed to happen all at once. From my right, I was immediately tackled. A burly man in some sort of uniform knocked the air out of my lungs. My face was pushed against the hard concrete, and several pairs of hands held me down and handcuffed me.

My eyes rolled around, and I struggled to see what was happening. From my vantage point, I could barely distinguish the bright yellow letters "SWAT" emblazoned across jackets. I didn't even have time to cry out.

They hauled me away in front of my cousin, who they left sitting in the truck. Deep down, I realized my time had finally come. I would only fully know the sensation of sinking, of the horrible, painful realization that I had finally been caught, that my past had caught up with me. No way could I go back to what I was before; I could not escape my fate, barrelling toward me with all the ferocity of an oncoming train.

They took me to the local station for processing. It was, as they say, an "open and shut" case. I was charged with "being a part of a group of five or more willing to commit a felony"—being part of a gang, in other words.

Normally, all of our gang meetings were conducted shirtless. That was to ensure that no one wore a police wire to record us. We also recorded our own personal notes, activities, and gang code names into a notebook; that was how you "leveled up" in a gang. You had to prove what you had done and know how the gang is run. We all had one.

"Billy" had one such notebook too. At the time, Billy was only a teenager. When his parents found his notebook, they immediately hauled him to the police station, ready to set him straight before he got caught doing other crimes. Needless to say, he turned informant; he would escape prison time in exchange for infiltrating our ranks, wearing a wire, and providing all the information he could about our whereabouts, dealings, and future plans. In one fateful meeting, we decided not to go shirtless; "Billy" could then record all of us. The police had enough evidence for a solid conviction. Up until then, I had been arrested 15 times; I had 15 other pending charges. They told me that they would drop all the additional charges against me if I pleaded guilty to this charge. Since I was third in command of the entire state, they had caught a pretty big fish, so to speak. They just wanted a conviction.

And that's what they got.

Fifteen Years Later...

As I sit in an Indiana prison, I quickly understand my "purpose" for entering this Correctional Facility. It hits me with the impact of an F5 tornado. My body goes limp, and it's all I can do to seize the tears from running down my face. Time no longer had meaning as it once did just seconds before. What the hell have I done to my life? What must I do to clutch the meaning of prison?

The journey I was about to embark on was simple, like an on-and-off switch. My attire that February morning consisted of a dark green suit, wet from the cold rain, white crew socks that have no reason of being matched up with any suit for that matter, and a brand new pair of dress shoes from a local department store.

I'm sure the on-lookers in the courtroom would be expecting some outburst from me by now, like kicking the chair legs, throwing papers off the table, or yelling out loud at my attorney. I didn't do any of those things; I don't think I did anything. My body was too unfeeling from the sentence given to me to react in any way but silence.

The guard, slightly taller than me and three years younger, put a new shiny pair of handcuffs on me and led me out of the courtroom to my new destination. My sentence, now compiled of Indiana laws that I had broken, gave ample reason to foresee the punishment given to me. For the first time in the history of our small town, a person was incarcerated for Criminal Gang Activity.

After a short trip down an elevator, up a flight of stairs, and across a busy street, we arrived suddenly and very unpredictably at the booking area at the county jail. The cold air was a scary reminder that I would not return home anytime soon. The bitterness of the wind pierced through my newly unworn suit as I placed one foot in front of the other, walking through a rainstorm.

After a briefing on what to do in the case of an attack or a rape on myself occurred, I was fingerprinted and dressed in a dark blue jumpsuit much different than the suit I previously wore. Nearly ten minutes later, I was shuffled down a lighted hall and placed into what I considered a tomb for humans.

My sentence was opposed that unearthly morning to one year in prison for my unkind acts of violence against others. The young nobody of a guard boasted that I would never make it in here and that I was never going home countless times throughout the day. I snapped back by referring him to my past life, "I have my own life, and I am stronger than you know, asshole!"

However, I carried the feeling that I was a dead man walking. I thought the streets that produced me into the monster that I had become. That night was the loneliest night of my human existence here on earth. My belongings were forced into a small locker until my release date.

I had the ungodly privilege of sitting in an 8-by-10-foot cell alone and hungry. With my past involvements with the wrong crowd and being a part of other things, I knew that I would turn it around or die here! Nothing else was an option. I was heading nowhere fast.

I had already failed with my work, schooling, and, most of all, myself. I had totally self-destructed in the course of one year. After a last-ditch effort to learn from my past, a pastor came into my cell to talk with me about my past life, childhood, and past associations, only then to leave after I spit into his face.

Many people asked me then, "How did you let yourself go, how did you end up in jail?"]

"When my father and my mother forsake me, then the Lord will take care of me." (Psalm 27:10, NKJV)

What they all wanted to know was if this could happen to them. I often always answer yes; this can happen to you before they even ask. Everyone I have known has hit bottom or knows someone that is hitting bottom presently. I was at the bottom.

So many wrongs had yet to be righted in my life. I came from a poorer-than-most upbringing, with a father who spent most of his life in street fights and at night in bars with different women.

This probably isn't the same cell I was in seven times before, but they are all the same to me; the same big steel gray door, a little window so you can only see a lit-up hallway, and two other grubby-looking inmates. These small cells are made for only two inmates. However, because of overcrowding, we were forced to pile three of us into the confines of a space no longer than eight by twelve feet.

I *hate* this place; the brick walls, metal bars, and child molesters next door always disgusted me. Everyone here stinks, and not an inch of the air moves causing you to smell everything. As you glance out the little window toward the hallway, another inmate might be *shitting* on the metal toilet right next to you.

After a few days, this dirty cell I am in empties out, and other inmates return home. I won't be one of those men. In fact, I won't be going home for a year after my conviction for *gang activity*. I can't believe I got arrested eight times in just three months. My chest tightened after the fourth day; my heart beat faster than ever before from withdrawal from heroin. I wrote gang signs on the cell walls and watched the small TV to pass the hours. My court-appointed lawyer always warned me about staying out of trouble, but I didn't care. I didn't care about anything.

Now this dumb, overpaid government lawyer who had never even met me before had pleaded me guilty to a felony gang charge. I had no intention of ever staying out of trouble. I at least had a warm place to stay out of the Indiana winter.

Before this jail cell, I lived on the streets in Indiana. The winter demonstrated a fall of over two feet of fresh snow. It would be another year before I touch the outside and the green grass.

Let my sentence come forth from their presence; let thin eyes behold the things that are equal ~Psalms 17:2

I *grasped* the prison bars in my upper cell to see if my feet would clear the floor, just in case I decided to end my life. Time at that point no longer moved forward. My imagination played tricks on me because of solitary confinement for 23 hours daily.

I heard voices from within the walls. I heard my mother in there telling me to stop writing. I heard my father in there saying I have to leave. I soon started questioning myself, what did I do so horribly wrong in my life to end up here bunking with murderers and child molesters? The noise in there was mind-blowing, and privacy was non-existent. Two months passed, and I began to see no hope of a release date.

At that point, it had been over 6,000 hours since the last visit from anyone. My money for food had run out, and the nights were filled with dismay. I can hardly bear this nightmare any longer. Two weeks ago, a childhood friend hung himself *two cells over* from where I slept. Minutes seemed like hours, and hours seemed like days in there.

On Tuesdays evenings, a pastor would come to our cell block and talk with the "believers" of our group. Only two had the courage to listen to what this short, old-looking pastor had to say about Jesus that was going to save us all.

I didn't want to hear anything about that nonsense. I shouted at the pastor, "Yeah if God is real like you say, Why did he put me in this prison?" The pastor built the courage to respond to me with, "Maybe he is preparing you for something Mr. Gaines! Here's a Bible, you might find your answer in there Chad." I just lowered my head and thought to myself, nonsense.

Moreover, that answer would come a few weeks later. For the next couple of weeks, other inmates left their cells for the prison library for books and communication with the women's cell block next to the library. I only had a sixth-grade education, so I didn't read well. I always remained in my eight-by-twelve-foot cell, thinking about how I could end my life day after day. I was at the end of my line. The only way out was in a *casket*, I thought. I planned to use my sheet on my bunk after our cells were on lockdown after 11 pm.

Due to the hanging of my elementary school friend, inmates were counted every hour, 24 hours a day, like we were cattle. That meant if I were to end my life in my cell, I had to do it between when the guard first counted us to when he came back at the top of the hour. I heard keys jingling from the hallway, which meant it was almost locked down for the night. Ten minutes later, we hear, "Lockdown, lights out animals!" The TV goes off, and we are ordered to go into our cells as the cell doors slam shut. A very upsetting sound every night for the last four months.

I walk into my cell and write a few lines at my little table. I glance at the Bible the pastor gave me as a cockroach crawls across the cover. I look away. I wait until I hear the courthouse bells from across the street chime at midnight because I know the guard will be in at any time to count us. I heard other inmates snoring. The guard opened our cell block to count us. He shined his light into our cells and counted as silently as possible. He closed out my cell, and I went into action, knowing I had an hour to end my life and talk myself out of it.

I take the sheet off my bunk and stand on my table. I was really going to do this, I thought silently. I tied one end of the bed sheet around my neck to the position needed to end my life and the other to the upper bars of my cell. I stood there on top of that table for what seemed to be hours with the bed sheet around my neck, knowing if I walked off this table in less than a minute, my horrible pain and life of anguish would be over for good, and I could just rest.

Stepping Off

With my last breath, I stepped off the prison table. My arms swing around like a ragdoll as I grab the sheets to get free. I kick my legs against the prison bars hoping to wake the inmates. My breath is short, and I am dying quickly. I can feel my air being sucked from my body as I continue to swing and kick for the little life I have left.

I can feel my eyes start to roll back in my head. Some sort of fluid comes from my mouth as life goes blank. Suddenly, I opened my eyes with puzzlement. Not understanding why I am looking under my bunk, and I have the biggest headache of my 26 years on this planet, I whisper, "Am I dead? I'm still here in my cell." I look down at my prison clothing and the fluid running from my mouth. I understood the bed sheet must have come loose, and I fell to the cement and hit my head. Now I'm looking straight under my bunk at some book that I never noticed there before this day. I reached for it; it had no cover, and I had to whip off the dust from it to see the title, "Twice Pardoned."

I sat up with the bed sheet still attached to my neck, thinking, damn, I can't even kill myself properly. What a damn failure, I thought. What does this mean now? What's next? I stand to my feet; my legs feel so weak—my head pounds from the long fall to the cement. I disentangle the sheet from my neck and throw it to my bunk. Why is this happening? I glance at that Bible and wonder for a moment if that crazy answer is why this so-called *God* won't let me die. Then, without thinking, I shout out loud, "It's my free will!" Other inmates yell back, "Shut the hell up, man!" I remain silent in hopes no one finds out what happened. I step toward the Bible, never opening one before in my life. I pick it up and put it back down. What the hell am I thinking? I'm not going to find an answer in some book I can't even understand or read, I tell myself.

Something draws me back to it. I whisper, "Ok, God, if you're so real, then talk to me man. Let me read something here so I can believe." Not knowing where to start or how to understand this Bible and what I might see there, I open it to a random page and read the first thing I see in the middle of the page. I read it and closed it as quickly as I opened it. What the heck was that? No way! I began to look around, waiting for the joke to be over and the cameramen to come out laughing at me, joking about how they punked me. However, that never happened; nothing but silence is all I heard that cold Indiana night in February. Alone I opened it again and reread it. The same page, the same message. For the first time in my life, I opened a Bible, and this is what I read.

Psalm 102 19-20 For he hath looked down from the height of his sanctuary; from heaven did the Lord behold the earth; To hear the groaning of the prisoner; to loosen those that are appointed to death.

My eyes were simply in disbelief from what I read there that night. I couldn't ignore it for some blunder, mistake, or purpose. I didn't know what to do next, but I knew somehow this God, this Jesus, was communicating with me through this Bible.

I drifted off to sleep on my unmade bunk. The next morning, the same thing happened: the cell doors opened at 6 am, letting its animals out. Dry cereal sets on our large table for breakfast. I whip last night's sleep out of my eyes, trying to figure out what the hell happened. That morning, the eight of us inmates ate in silence. Almost a calming peace overtook our space inside that cell block. The usual mornings there were somewhat like this; we ate cold cereal and went back to our bunks to read or sleep some more. That morning was different. Tim did push-ups, Danny wrote a letter to his wife on the outside, and I wanted to look at the book I found under my bunk after I fell to the cement.

I finished breakfast that morning and returned to my cell to discover that book I had wondered about. I turned to the first page and realized I couldn't read most of the words due to my lack of education. I was upset about the recent happenings of last night, and now I couldn't even read this book that was placed under my bunk. The day passed and became night once again. I paced back and forth in my little cell after lockdown. Over and over again, I walked that cell–eight steps from the wall to my cell door and back again for the next three hours straight in only a pair of shorts and holding a blank yellow notebook that my lawyer gave me to write on. I had another *six months* to think about my life and what I would do upon my release.

I began to study the American Directory from the prison library to learn new words like integrity, diligence, and edify. That Directory was my magic tool to break away from where I was locked up physically. However, I was a prisoner without those bars surrounding me. After about a week of learning to read my Directory on a different level than ever, a visitor left me a gift after inmates were locked down. That night after we were in our cells, I began nightly writing about my feelings. The guard came in for his second night check, so I knew it must be after 1 am. This time was much different than all the other times before. As always, he would open the door, shine the light in our cells, count inmates, and then close the door. This time, he opened our door and walked up the stairs to my cell. I was writing about the thoughts that I had at the time. The guard reaches into my cell through the bars and lays down a razor blade. I look at him and whisper, "What's this for?" He replies, "Do it right this time, Gaines." I look at him in shock. He whispers back, "Someone is always *watching* in this place. I'll skip the next hourly check so you can finish up the job you started two weeks ago with those bed sheets." The guard walks back down the stairs and closes our cell door. I sat there looking at the razor blade. Someone in here hopes I'll kill myself.

I stand to my feet with the razor blade in my right hand, walk over to the toilet, and flush it down. I sat back down and began reading my first book, "Twice Pardoned." As time passed and I reached chapter two, I realized the author's story was much like my life. He got involved in drinking, ran with the "wrong crowd," and ended up in prison. In his case, his associates led him to two counts of murder. His prison sentence was two life sentences with no chance of parole. He passed out in the backseat of a car driven by two of his friends. The car stops at a liquor store; two men walk into the store, leaving their friend passed out in the backseat of the car. The two men robbed and killed both people working in the store. He wakes up at the shouts of his friends yelling, "Drive, drive, drive!" Days later, he would be arrested for two counts of first-degree murder. As I read this book, I started to feel that my life wasn't so bad. A suggestion was told to me many years ago: if you want to feel better about your life, listen to someone's story, which is more messed up than yours. It's a funny suggestion but very true in how we think today.

That next night for the first time, I bent down at my prison door to talk to the pastor. He didn't preach or tell me what I should have done on the outside, so I didn't end up here. All he said was, tell me about yourself, Chad. I didn't know how to answer him. No one in my life had ever asked me that question. I almost found myself stuttering as I did in the second grade as a scared little boy. He looked at me and said, "Believe me or not, Chad, God has a *purpose* for your life, and it's not in this prison."

He asked me things like, What would I do when I got out? Where was I going to go? What kind of job was I going to work? I didn't really think of those things while inside that cell. *Solitary confinement* can make a man lose his mind in so many ways. I just stood, not saying anything. It had always been instilled in me that I wouldn't amount to anything I said. The pastor snapped back, "You're meant to do so much in this life. Just wait." Again, I said nothing to him. He said, "I believe you can help change so many people around this area so they don't end up here like you." That night I sat at my table inside that cell pondering my life and what would happen next.

I began to read my book. The first book I would thoroughly read in my twenty-six years of life. I read how after this author ended up in prison, he gave his life to Jesus. What did giving your life to Jesus even mean? It meant, to him, that he gave up on his life and turned it over to Jesus. I didn't understand how all that worked. In fact, I had never prayed before.

The author talked about his *former* life and how he didn't want to live like that any longer. That sounded a lot like me. I was getting tired of the gang and drug life. They said "they" were going to always be there for you. I looked at the wall in my cell, I looked left, and I looked back to the right. I didn't see anyone else doing this prison time with me. It was the middle of summer by now. I thought, what would I be doing if I was on the *outside*? I thought most likely high or drunk. After more than seven months, that life no longer sounded too exciting. I wanted to do something different. I thought, purpose, huh?

My mind that night raced in so many different directions. One minute I was back in my seven-year-old body and my mother yelling in my face, and the next, writing about my life in some book. I pictured my own book in bookstores and doing great things to help others. I knew if I were ever to do something to that level, my life would be in danger. I wondered, am I crazy for thinking about me, the little boy from a town of population 500 in the middle of nowhere, writing some book?

That night in that little cell, I stood from my writing table and walked to the middle of my cell around 2 am and fell to my knees and said these words: "God, If *you're* real and will give me a chance, I'll go wherever you want me to go. I don't know if you can forgive someone like me that has hurt so many, used drugs, been drunk more times than I can remember, and is now a prisoner. Please, God, forgive me for these things. Please, God." My body felt weird. It felt like I was getting shocked. I thought for a moment God was about to strike me down for asking him for forgiveness. I didn't want that life anymore. I had never talked to God before that night.

The following day, I woke up excited and wasn't sure why. The walls were the same. The prison bars remained, but my reaction to my surroundings was different now. I found beauty in those other inmates. I guess you have a different heart, approach, and walk when you surrender. I was excited about *knowledge,* and I spent every minute left of my prison term learning about my life before and what I wanted to do after I was released. I read the Book of Job and his terrifying journey from loss to disease to faith and returning everything a hundredfold. I could no longer sit by with my life and ignore this story. I thought to myself, is this my fate? Would there still be more I would have to face?

The pastor asked me to put together a plan of action: a list of ten things I would do once I was released in the next 90 days. That became a challenging list for me. I once thought all I wanted to do when I got out of that cell was to party and hang out. Now my mindset was, how could I help others get away from gangs and drugs? I met with the pastor on Tuesday with my list of ten things I wanted to acknowledge and accomplish. That Tuesday was the first night I saw this little, old pastor light up excitedly in nearly four months.

He gleamed with joy and excitement in his voice. "I think you're onto something here, Chad. You want to help and serve now." I replied, "Yes!" "Where do I start, I ask?" He explained how he could most likely get me into a church to share my testimony. I trembled with a bit of fear and replied, "You mean to talk in front of people? I don't think I can do that, ever!" "Well, it could help others," he said. For the next few nights, I lay in my bunk in the tiny cell going back and forth between myself and God. I wavered between how I would walk on a stage and talk about my life and how I wanted others to be inspired by my new life.

I must have gone back and forth over a hundred times in those four nights there

Job 1;3 At this, Job got up and tore his robe and shaved his head. Then he fell to the ground in worship.

And with that, I began my journey to go wherever God would lead me. The pastor walked me through how I needed to prepare for that statement I had made to go wherever God would lead me. That will be a challenging *journey* and path. He described a journey for strength and an unshakeable faith. He said, "People that you don't even know will come against you. Also, people that don't even know you will support your journey. It's' something about passion that will lead you forward onto the next project for God."

August 2000

Some of the best words my ears have ever heard came from a prison guard. It was during the hot summer of 2000. We all lived through the W2K event. My cell block door opened, and in one sentence, my life was changed, "Gaines get all your shit together, you're going home!"

I ran to my cell and began to pack my stuff. I yelled out, "I'm going home!" I was about to walk to my freedom for the first time in a year. I wondered, at the time, what would the green grass look like? After rolling up my mat, I got dressed in my street clothes, which no longer fit, and was given my $32 in my commissary money and walked to the front door by the guard. The bright sun and green were the most exciting things I had seen in over a year.

Ten minutes ago, I was filled with excitement. Now my excitement has changed to fear of what to do now. It's not like companies will knock on my door, offering me a job somewhere. I felt excited but defeated. On the first night of my release, I stayed inside and away from my old group of *friends*. I studied how to talk differently, dress better, and where I could share my story on stage anywhere I was needed. It didn't take long. That first Tuesday of my release, my phone rang. A broken voice on the other end of the phone said, "Is this Chad Gaines?" I replied, "Yes, sir, this is Chad!"

"I don't know if you remember me, but I visited you in jail. I am the pastor." "I remember you of course", I said. My face probably lit up from excitement. The pastor asked if I would keep my promise and speak at his church. My body went into this weird shock of fear and excitement. I couldn't explain what was happening to me. Before I could think of an answer, I repeated, "Yes sir, yes sir!" "Good," he replied. "Are you ready this Sunday?"

I quickly replied, "Yes I am ready to go on stage!" I hung up the phone in disbelief. I went to the mirror that night to gather enough *courage* to face the people I once terrorized as a criminal. I was facing that fork in the road or, in my case, the no turning back once I shared my story on that stage. The next day I found myself at a local Goodwill looking for a suit to wear for Sunday. With my $32 from jail, I bought my suit for $15 and went to get a haircut. I felt like a new man. I survived through many things I thought to get here. *I hadn't seen anything yet.*

The church parking lot didn't even have the space for all the cars. More than 264 people were there that day. Being scared doesn't give justice to the real feeling I had that morning in August. In life, the past is never far. I couldn't turn back now. The church was so packed that some stood in the back to listen. I'm looking at myself in the bathroom mirror. I'm trying to understand how and why I am supposed to do what I'm about to do. Am I crazy? I wondered. Why am I thinking bad thoughts? It was almost like I was back home listening to my mother's humiliating words. I began to listen, and she told me, "You're just some little boy with a *big fuckin' dream* Chad Richard! You need to get a real job and stop talking about this!"

I finally snapped out of it. It was just me, without help, standing in front of that mirror. I wondered about a lot of things. I questioned everything. I was trying to answer questions that I didn't have answers to. I looked at myself in the mirror and whispered slowly, quietly, "Not today." I walked out of the bathroom wearing my oversized $15 suit from Goodwill and was about to speak for the first time on a stage. My body felt like I was gaining a hundred pounds with every step I took toward the stage. By the time I did arrive at the bottom of the steps, I was covered in sweat.

I automatically felt like that 7-year-old boy. I felt trapped and all alone in a house filled with horrific events happening to me. Those three steps that I took that day up to the stage were the most significant steps of my entire life at that time.

"The people that have gathered here today are the same people that I once terrorized," I said. I terrorized many of them with violence. Many others here, I once terrorized with theft. "I'm simply here today to share my story of who I was and who I want to be in the future." Some clapped. Some just sat in silence. Some moved around in their seats as if it was too much to hear now.

Some things in this life you can't change. I walked off that stage feeling so defeated by my past mistakes. I didn't know what to think or where I would go after today. Some events won't be explained until you go through them. God is cool like that. Just as I stepped down the stairs from the stage that morning, I was greeted by a warm smile. The tall man walked toward me with a question. "Hi, Chad! My name is Bill. I can really relate to your story. My brother and I went through some horrible things at the hands of our dad. Now, I work as a professor at a university up north. Have you ever thought about sharing at a university?" I thought for a quick second or two. I said, "I never really thought about it." Bill replied, "Would you share your story at the University?" I said, "Wherever God wants me to go, I'll go." Bill smiled and took my phone number for a later call.

Nearly two weeks later, I got the call of a lifetime. Bill called me to ask if I would speak at the University. The only problem was I didn't know where this University was or know how many people I would be speaking to. At this time of my release, I am 28 years old. What I was about to hear would change my life and launch a speaking career. Bill explained, "You'll be speaking at the *University of Notre Dame*. There will most likely be a little over *4,000 students* and professors."

Telling you that I was in shock is an understatement. I became silent and nearly hung up the phone. Then, after what seemed to be an hour, which was only about 3-4 seconds, I answered back. I stuttered a few times on the phone like I once did in elementary school. "I'll be there on Tuesday night." And just like some magic trick, I began speaking to schools, churches, and anywhere else I could share my story.

As Tuesday evening approached, where I would speak to one of the greatest universities, the University of Notre Dame, I began to have doubts that I could measure up to these incredible students. I thought, what could I teach them? I'm 28, a felon, and have never been to any university.

Even as scared as I was, I knew I had to go. I remember walking on the stage covered in sweat in my $15 Goodwill suit. The lights on the stage were so hot they blinded me from seeing any of the students. After making a few corny jokes, I got right to the meat and potatoes of my life story. I didn't know where to start since I never spoke publicly.

I knew I had come so far, but I still had a very long road ahead of me. I knew nothing about business and managing money since I came from a lover-middle-class family in a little Indiana farm town.

I stood in front of nearly 4,000 students with a microphone in my left hand, and the palm on my right hand felt like it was on fire. My soul was on fire for speaking to people by then. I had finally understood what my calling was on this earth.

I began to speak with my scared little boy voice. I introduced myself and began sharing the days of the 1980s and the events that took place. I learned so many things that night on stage. I learned it takes courage to be that personal with so many strangers. I still couldn't tell you if it was courage or stupidity. I'd like to think it was more courage. That was the first time I was given a standing ovation in my upcoming speaking career.

I left that place on Tuesday night, excited and wondering where this may take me. I remember the hour-long drive back home from the University of Notre Dame. As I rode in the passenger seat, so many things flashed inside of my head, and so many voices from my mother troubled me. The words "you're not worthy to be here," crossed my mind several times that night. The car rides seemed much longer than the previous drives to South Bend, Indiana. I kept thinking, "Chad, you just spoke at one of the top universities in the country and you don't even have a college degree." I knew right then and there that night, in the car, that I wanted to do this for the rest of my life. I wanted to explain to people in a way that they could understand and relate and that not everyone comes from the perfect family with two parents. I never dreamed what would happen next. A little less than two weeks after I spoke at the University, I received over 300 emails wanting me to speak at their schools around the country.

I was totally in shock, and obviously, I didn't understand how universities really worked. In my small way of thinking, I just assumed everybody that went to the University of Notre Dame lives in South Bend. That was the first day that I discovered how universities work. I laugh about it now, yes. But I didn't understand back then that, obviously, not everybody attending the University of Notre Dame lives in South Bend. OK. Just stay with me on this one. OK? At the end of my speech or story or whatever label you want to put on it, they posted my email address on the scoreboard as students were leaving.

I thought it was cool. I did not understand that many students live around the country and go there for school. After they posted my email address on the scoreboard and suggested that if you would like to have Chad guest speak at your next function, please email him; two things were about to happen for me. The first thing, as I mentioned before, was my calling. I strongly felt somewhere in me that this is what I was called to do for the rest of my life. The second thing was the promise I made in prison to God: "I'll go wherever you want me to go if I get another chance." From within those 300 emails that I received, God sent me around the country to speak. Less than three weeks after I was released from prison, I traveled the whole country. I spoke at middle schools, high schools, universities, and juvenile justice centers from one coast to the next.

Nearly one year after I began my public speaking career, it became successful. It quickly took me from the east coast to the west coast, speaking anywhere I was asked to share. By the time 2001 came, I was feeling about where my life was headed. I had won many awards for overcoming insurmountable odds. I was now getting paid for sharing my life story with others. It had been a few months since I last spoke to my mother. I was trying hard to distance myself from the family. They would often send threats about me, "speaking about things I had no business speaking about."

So many things happened in my home. I never wanted to mention a few things in this book or interviews, but it weighed heavy on my heart. I have seen it in my dreams when I slept at night. The hot summer of 2001 forever changed my life and exposed a *family secret*.

I couldn't have more than a 5-minute conversation with my mother. By now, anything longer than 5 mins, we would begin to tussle between words of disrespect. There seemed to be this power struggle between wanting to talk about these things and not wanting to die because of them. The threats became real and more straightforward as time went on. But, on the road speaking, I felt that's where I belong. I had so much passion for people when I was on stage.

Early Morning July 20, 2001

What I am about to talk about in this section of my book, took me nearly three years to write. I battled for some time with that little boy inside of me to talk about this. Now as a 28-year-old man, I was trying to put my terrible past behind me to gain some control over the abuse and how it affected me daily, even today. The early morning phone would change my life.

My phone: Ring, Ring, Ring, Ring, Ring, Ring!

Finally, after the sixth ring, I picked the receiver up. Hello? On the other end of the line is my mother with a single sentence. "Chad, I think I just killed Rick! There was foam coming out of his mouth!" I sat up in bed as she dropped the phone. *Rick* was a man she dated on and off through the years after my dad left. They were only married a few months prior to this phone call. I leaped out of bed in shorts and a white T-shirt. I made the three-block run barefoot to her house to see what she had done this time.

I ran up to her trailer and noticed their blue van was parked outside. I saw two state police cars and one county police car parked in their drive-around. As I made it to the front stairs, I was stopped by an officer asking who I was. My mother was sitting on a living room chair with a blank stare. I was frightened by the look on her face. I sat across from her on the loveseat. The six police officers gathered in the bedroom with Rick's lifeless body. The officers found over 100 full and empty bottles of pain medicine that morning.

As I sit on the loveseat across from my mother, The coroner walks through the trailer's front door. A clear sign that Rick was dead in the next room. My mind went in so many directions with what happened. I wondered, "How can Rick be dead when he's only 38?" He was only ten years older than I was.

So many different questions I wanted to ask my mother. She was sitting in her big chair in the living room, shaking her leg back and forth in a panic. She didn't talk. The officers and the coroner were still in the bedroom with the body. Several minutes passed, and the six officers and the coroner opened the bedroom door carrying Rick's body in a bedsheet. I was so in disbelief that they were carrying a dead body right in front of me. Finally, when everyone was outside the trailer, my mother began to tell me the details of what happened that evening. I wanted to know what took place deep into the middle of the night.

With the six officers outside, she began to tell me in graphic detail what had happened that night. She also told me where she went after she called 911. She began to tell me that she filled up one of his syringes that he used for his diabetes with a drug that they were using the night before, which she never disclosed to me. She said it was some pills they crushed up and cooked on the stove to make it a liquid. She put it in the syringe and shot it into his lower back while he was sleeping. She said, "I woke up at about 2 am. Foam was coming out of his mouth." She panicked and ran to the kitchen and called my grandmother. My grandmother told her that she needed to get those guns out of the house that were in her name because Rick was a federal felon and wasn't supposed to be around guns. She went over to my grandmother's and hid all their guns downstairs in the basement. On her way back home, I received her phone call saying she thought she killed Rick. Somewhere between when she left my grandmother's and when she called me, she called 911 to tell them that she thought her husband was dead. Where her story went wrong was when the officers arrived before she got back home, and it was reported in the newspaper article that this was an unattended death.

Sometime that morning, Rick's sister was informed of his death. There was significant conflict between my mother, his sister, and his mother. My mother demanded that his body be cremated immediately to cover up her actions. The last thing in the world she wanted was an autopsy to be done. Several days passed without a conclusion on whether to bury or cremate him. Finally, my mother decided to let his mother make the final decision and take the punishment for what she had done. After the autopsy was performed, it showed that his heart had exploded. It took them nearly a month for burial because he was so large that they did not have a casket his size in the state of Indiana. They eventually buried him in a vault. And soon after, this case and the death of Rick were closed and never discussed.

Cause of Death:

26 PART I Enter the diseases, injuries or complications that caused the death. Do not enter terminal events such as cardiac or respiratory arrest, shock or heart failure. List only one cause on each line.				Approximate interval between onset and death
IMMEDIATE CAUSE (Final disease or condition resulting in death)	. Arteriosclerotic Heart Disease			Years
	DUE TO (OR AS A CONSEQUENCE OF)			
Conditions, if any, which give rise to the immediate cause, stating the underlying cause last	b ___			
	DUE TO (OR AS A CONSEQUENCE OF)			
	c ___			
	DUE TO (OR AS A CONSEQUENCE OF)			
	d			
PART II Other significant conditions - Conditions contributing to death but not resulting in the underlying cause given in Part I	27) WAS DECEDENT PREGNANT OR 90 DAYS POSTPARTUM? (Yes or no)	28a WAS AN AUTOPSY PERFORMED? (Yes or no)	28b WERE AUTOPSY FINDINGS AVAILABLE PRIOR TO COMPLETION OF CAUSE OF DEATH? (Yes or no)
Diabetes Mellitus , Morbid Obesity Hypertensive Cardiovascular Disease	No	Yes	YES

Six months after what she had done to Rick, she began to talk about it to many different friends of hers. It was almost like she was bragging about what she got away with. I remember that morning of his death; she said a few strange things to me. She first mentioned that she was going to prison for the rest of her life. Then, she threatened me that I would never be found again if I ever talked about it. I took her with me to the church to talk to the youth pastor about what happened. In front of me, she confessed to this youth pastor what she had done and asked for forgiveness. The same youth pastor would be the officiating pastor at Rick's funeral.

I know all the records and facts of this case are still there, and the evidence will lead the authorities to make the right decision and change his death certificate to murder. I'm not asking anything from this case other than to make this right. So many people around the town were horrified by my family and their violence. My mother went on with her life, moved in with my grandmother, and often spoke about what she had done to many of her friends. Yet, somewhere in my heart, I believe that my stepfather, Rick, deserves justice for what happened to him. So in my own words, I'm asking you, the reader, and the public, if you will help me bring attention to this case. And by this, make the wrong, right, and bring justice for Rick.

Fork in the Road

Between public speaking engagements, I worked part-time at a chain restaurant as a waiter. While I was there, I met a lady who was the bartender. She was friendly and personable, and something about her made me open up. I would share bits and pieces about my story, childhood, home life, and what I had been through. Waiting on tables could be stressful—working with people generally was, and I needed to talk. She was an exceptional listener, as most good bartenders tend to be.

What I didn't know was that she was going home and telling her husband about my story. He was involved in the local chapter of the United States Junior Chamber—JC or "Jaycees" for short. I didn't know it then, but this organization did—and does—a lot of community work like park or lake clean-ups, fundraiser hosting, and things of that nature.

One day, her husband comes to pick her up from work. I wouldn't have noticed, except he approached me that day.

"Hello, Mr. Gaines?" he said.

I stopped wiping down a table, conscious of my waiter's apron in front of a man who wore a nice-looking suit. "Yes?"

He extended his hand. "I'm from the local chapter of Junior Commerce. Every year the organization holds an award ceremony for the top ten young Americans who exemplify courage, leadership, and potential." I nodded along, unsure where exactly he was going.

He motioned to his wife. "I hope you don't mind, but my wife has been sharing a bit of your story with me, and I've got to say that you've lived such an incredible life, and have made it through some pretty difficult circumstances."

Heat prickled across the back of my neck; imagine if someone approached you saying that they knew about all the horrible things that have happened to—and because of—you.

"That's why I would like to nominate you for this award. There's no guarantee, but I wanted to ask if that would be OK with you."

"Um," I said eloquently. "Sure."

"Great," he replied. We talked briefly afterward, and he summarized my information and life until that point.

"Now, I don't want to get your hopes up. There's usually several thousands of people nominated, and they only pick ten in all of America," he said before he left.

I said OK, and he left. I was excited for a few days. I had never been nominated for any award before, and it was pretty neat. Then, I put it out of my mind. At the time, I had no idea what the award was, how big of a deal it was, or who some of the past winners were—like Elvis Presley or Christopher Reeve, my childhood hero. While most people would have been thrilled just to be nominated, I didn't allow myself to get excited over something that might not happen. My mother's voice hissed in my mind— "Who do you think you are to win an award? What makes you so special?"

Better, I reasoned, to not get my hopes up so I wouldn't be disappointed.

Then, I got an email from the head of the National JayCees.

"Hello! I'm Sherry, and I just wanted to inform you that you made it to the top 1,000 applicants."

Still, my reaction was *OK, that's cool, nice if it happens*. I wasn't aware because I hadn't done any research. I was trying to pay attention to work and focus on making it through life.

But the emails kept coming. Top 100. Top 50. When I received a phone call that I had made it to the top 25 applicants, I finally started to ask questions. "What does it mean if I win? What's going to happen?" Then I started researching the award and realized it was much bigger than I thought.

John F. Kennedy won this award, I thought with some awe. But, as I read about past winners, it was not a sense of pride that washed over me, but of doubt, even shame.

How can I go onstage where I come from—a town of 500 people and be considered special?

My mother's voice resounded in my head: "This is not something you deserve. Who do you think you are?"

The more I thought, the more I considered turning down the award to give to someone worthier. Actors, politicians, and humanitarians had come before me. What had I done that was so unique, so worthy of being honored?

I wasn't worthy, I concluded. It was just a mistake. Surely, it was some clerical error. I would call them and sort everything out.

But I didn't. I was already working hard during the week as a server and taking on speaking events on the weekends, so I put the award firmly out of my mind.

Finally, on a busy Friday night, I received a call. It was so hectic—servers running to and fro from the kitchen, pots, and pans clanking, and chefs yelling orders were ready. Sherry—the head of the chapter of the Jaycees—called me.

"Chad, I'm very happy to say that you have officially been honored as one of the 10 outstanding young Americans," she said.

"That's great, Sherry, but I'm really busy," I replied. Then, I heard someone call my name and told her that I needed to hang up. I still had no clue about how big the award was. I was just focused on my work.

"Alright, I understand, but we need to send you to a place to get fitted for a suit because you'll have to wear a tux."

"OK, thank you." Then I hung up. Fitted? Tux? Just what exactly was this award? I imagined it would be held in a school auditorium or maybe a community center in Indiana.

I threw myself back into work for the night, again putting the award out of my mind. It still hadn't fully hit me. Most people would have been jumping for joy, calling all their friends, or at the very least, having their mouths open in shock. It wasn't that I took it for granted—far from it; part of me couldn't accept that I had won.

Less than 60 days after that, I was in a horrible car wreck that would change my life forever.

Miracle In The Water

The Indiana winters are bizarre and bitterly cold at times throughout the winter. Oftentimes, there was blowing snow and ice on the roads. Their winters are famous for deep cold and heavy snow. Many times, the temperatures in Indiana were below zero. My new job required me to work the evening shifts from 5 pm to 11 pm, sometimes even after. This cold evening was no different from others. As I left work, I was so tired that my eyes burned from fatigue. All I wanted was to get home, eat something hot, and fall asleep in a nice, warm bed.

The night was dark, with stars blinking at me. My breath fogged in front of my face. As I walked out to my car, I slid on the ice. I swore as my feet slipped out, and I landed hard on my tailbone. I should have paid more attention to that warning sign that the ice was slippery—and invisible.

I carefully picked myself up, my nose already numb, just from being outside for a few minutes. It was the kind of cold that made your lungs hurt. As I stood up, I figured that I bruised my tailbone. Unfortunately, that's not uncommon in this area during winter.

I turned on the engine and let my car warm up about 20 minutes before the 35-minute drive home. I cranked on the heater to full blast, and my eyes closed as my body warmed up.

The temperature in the car was 8 degrees Fahrenheit. I yawned, wishing I was already home. It was one of those nights when the trip seemed to take forever; I didn't know I would have a sudden, violent detour.

I put the car in reverse, then began my long, cold journey home. As I surveyed the ground, I thought *we probably had 3 inches of snow*. My route took me down a county road for a 35-minute drive back home. It was very late by this time, most likely around 1:30 am. My entire body aches—just another normal closing night at work. But tonight was about to prove that this was not a regular night.

To keep myself awake, I turned on the radio to hear Ruben Studdard sing, "Sorry 2004."

It happened in the blink of an eye. Only later would I figure out what happened. My car hit a patch of black ice, nearly invisible on the road. My eyes closed briefly, but it was all it took.

The sound of metal tearing off my car was earsplitting and discordant, like a banshee wail. Suddenly, my car began to roll over and over.

I screamed. I was just a rag doll being tossed around, strapped only by my seat belt.

Confusion mixed with fear. I clenched the steering wheel.

At that time, it felt like an episode of *The Twilight Zone*. I had entered some bizarre, violent world that I didn't understand. I could still hear the music and Ruben Suddard crooning over the sounds of breaking glass and crunching metal. It felt surreal hearing the radio. Normalcy clashed with the deadly.

Over and over, I spun.

I couldn't figure out if I was alive or dead. The car just kept spinning. I counted to myself every time the car went upside down, nine times total. And then one final time, end over end. While I was being tossed, I had sudden, visceral flashes. I would never make it to the Top Ten Young Americans Award Ceremony. I had so much left to do, to accomplish. My mother's face was leering at me. All the while, glass shattered, and metal tore, shrieking.

Then I heard nothing but the dark silence. I still didn't know if I was alive or dead. Both hands were still clutched to the steering wheel. My heart pounded in my mouth. My chest heaved, and my horrible pain bloomed in my head. Blood rushed to my head, and it took me a second to realize that I was upside down. The car's roof lay on the ground, and the tires pointed toward the sky, spinning in futile motion.

I was dizzy from being tossed like clothes in a dryer, and everything in front of my eyes still spun, though I was still.

For a moment, at least.

Then, the car started to creak again. Even though it was upside down, it began to move, sliding down a hill on its roof.

And suddenly, I heard the horrible sound of ice breaking, but I didn't know what the sound was.

Then something cold and wet touched me, and with horror, I realized that my whole car was filling up with water. Fast. And I was still upside down with my seatbelt on.

I scrabbled and clawed at my belt, but I was hooked. My saving grace became the thing that would kill me. Water continued to rise, as did my panic. The cold of the water was shocking, and as I took one final breath, I cried out, "God, I don't want to die!"

Then the water closed over my head. I was completely submerged underwater.

Underneath the water, the only thing I could still see was the car's headlights. I yanked on my seat belt, but it didn't budge.

I closed my eyes one more time. I only felt the water's bone-numbing coldness and the seatbelt's rough texture against my skin.

Until something jerked on my left arm, like a tug, the next thing I know, I'm outside the car holding on to the bumper. I was still underwater, but I knew by feeling that I was outside of the car.

My lungs burned. Everything in me cried out for oxygen. For one second, I panic because I cannot see anything; I don't know which way is up.

I grabbed the bumper of my car a little tighter, and my hand burned. I yelped, losing precious air, and let go, realizing what I was holding on to was the radiator. I look up through the water and its complete darkness. I can't see anything and can't believe I'm still alive underwater. Or am I?

Then, I see a light in the water. I couldn't tell if it was still one of the headlights or if someone was flashing a light from above down to the water.

I was dizzy from a lack of oxygen. Should I follow the light? If it was coming from above, I would move to safety; if it was the car headlights, I would swim toward my death.

I closed my eyes for the final time underwater, and I sensed a cool flow of water, and the next thing I knew, I was standing on the country road I was driving in, 14 feet above the water. Air rushed into my lungs, and water streamed over my face. I took deep breaths, gulping air. I whipped around, trying to take in my surroundings.

How…?

I shivered. The cold was unforgiving.

That's when I saw my friend, Mark, walking down the country road, coming toward me. Even though I was elated, I couldn't figure out how this was possible. For one, it was 8 degrees outside, and Mark didn't even have a coat on. He just had a long-sleeved white shirt.

And secondly, Mark died over ten years ago.

All I could do was stare as he walked toward me. I considered that maybe I had died, and Mark was there to take me wherever he would lead.

He smiled when he arrived before me, though he never said a word. He held out his hand, and I took it. The wind cut me to the bone, but I felt safe with Mark there. I was out of the water. I was walking. My clothes clung to me as heavy as cement, but I didn't care.

Mark held my right hand, and we began to walk down the country road. His hand felt warm and comforting. I somehow put one foot in front of the other. If I had made it this far, I could make it a little more. Less than one mile away was a house with a porch light on. Seeing that light on gave me one of the best feelings ever. Its warm light beckoned to safety. I knew that was my only chance to get back home.

As Mark and I walked, I could feel the presence of 2 other people somewhere behind us. You know those times, when you can sense something is there behind you? I was having one of those moments but on a bizarre level. The feeling was so strong, then a gentle grasp on my left hand. I could feel somebody holding my left hand now. I was almost too afraid to turn around and see who it was as if I might make them disappear just by looking at them. I just felt so happy to see my best friend again. And I could feel somebody directly behind me, and I could sense how much taller they were. I was completely hemmed in, no longer alone. The terror I had felt underneath the water gradually subsided. We now moved as a group. Eventually, I glanced to my left. It was Bob. He and his wife used to babysit me in the early 1980s. I felt so happy to see him, the man I considered my father in name, if not in blood. My closest friends were right there with me, and I felt such a sense of peace and love. They guided me, but I still felt a strong presence behind me.

To my right was my best friend, Mark, whom I lost many years ago. At a certain point, we stopped while walking down the road. We all turned around at the same time. It wasn't so much curiosity that drove me as a feeling that I should just turn around and look. I knew someone was watching me, but it wasn't a creepy or suspenseful feeling, but more like you know how someone is on watch duty.

Directly behind me, what we all saw was Jesus. He didn't speak his name, but I knew it was Him. He appeared to be twenty feet tall. We could all feel a sense of peace and happiness emanating from him. We all didn't say a word; we didn't have to. It's just something that you can feel. As He looked up to the sky, we all seemed to be floating higher and higher.

And in a blink of an eye, it seemed like we were in a different location. Or maybe even a different planet. There were bright white clouds and a fence with a gate that was probably ten feet tall. It appeared to go for many, many miles. I didn't feel scared. I didn't feel happy. I didn't feel anything. And just as fast as this accident took place, it was over. I recall the feeling of falling with no emotions or feelings. Just falling. I blinked my eyes, and just like that, I was standing on somebody's porch, knocking on their door.

A lady answered and looked at me up and down.

"Are you OK?" she asked because it was around 2 am, and no stranger who knocked on a door in the middle of the night was ever really OK. "Are you from that car wreck? I heard about it on the radio."

"I am. May I come inside and warm up a little?"

She opened the door wider. "Oh my god, yes, of course. You know, in this area, there are tons of accidents year-round, not just in the winter, but even in the summertime. It's that damn curve. It gets people all the time." She spoke rapidly like she could keep the bad luck of a car accident away if she filled the silence.

She kept talking as I stepped over the threshold. The warm air from her heating unit felt so good on my skin and my face. Somehow, my clothes had dried, but I still shivered.

"Oh, can I get you something?"

"Just something hot to drink."

"Here's a blanket, too. Goodness, you must be chilled to the bone. It's cold enough to freeze Hell out there."

She bustled about the kitchen, and I stood in the living room, the surreal feeling washing over me. I was alive. I kept reminding myself of that, but it didn't seem accurate. I almost believed that I would wake up back underneath the car.

"Here you go." She handed me a steaming mug. "Is the driver dead?"

I shook my head and sipped, savoring the hot chamomile tea. It felt so good to hold something warm in my hands.

"Are you sure? If you left the car, then...oh my god, do we need to rescue the driver?" She grabbed her coat off the rack by the entrance.

"No, no. I was the driver. There was no one else."

The woman blinked. She then looked me up and down. "Are you joking? You don't even look like you were bruised. The radio said that there was glass and metal everywhere."

And I said, "No I'm not and I'm very serious."

Her mouth dropped open.

"And I don't know where my car is because it's somewhere underwater," I added.

She lifted one hand to her mouth and looked at me again like she was gauging whether I was lying. I supposed she believed me because she didn't say anything else.

She and her husband took me the rest of the way home that night.

As I arrived back home, I was completely silent about the events that just took place. As a matter of fact, I didn't speak about those events for nearly 20 years after.

But there was something that I took away from that accident. I realized how big my life was projected to be. For the first time, I saw myself not through other people's eyes but through my own. I saw how much I didn't want to lose. Everything was so much bigger and brighter after emerging from the car wreck—no broken bones, no scratches.

I couldn't believe it when I saw how badly smashed the car was.

Maybe, just maybe, if I survived, then that meant something. Maybe my life was worth something after all if I had survived being flipped nine times and near drowning.

I realized I was worthy of winning the Top Ten Young Americans award, and I could finally put all the guilt and shame my mother placed behind me. Her voice no longer ran so loudly in my mind.

The moment it finally hit me to be accepted as an award winner was when I was driving to a speaking engagement at a middle school. As my tires ate up the road under me, it finally clicked. For me, winning the award wasn't the end, like it might have been for some people but the beginning. Instead, it marked a turning point in how I needed to live my life. If other people thought I was unique enough and worthy enough of winning, I had to live up to it. I had to prove that I was worthy of carrying that torch. I couldn't just prop my feet up and live easily. I had to do things that most people won't do. Speak and help people. It was a quiet moment, but I was humbled and grateful.

Six months after that car accident that should have taken my life, I walked on stage in Tulsa, Oklahoma. I was then honored as one of the *Ten Outstanding Young Americans* in the country. But even then, it brought about a change I had never anticipated. And at first, it was terrifying.

Losing Control of Myself

When I landed in Tulsa, it was two days before the event. The award ceremony would be held in a Double Tree Inn.

I felt so out of place when I walked into my hotel room. Huge fruit baskets, flowers, and small gifts from different chapters of the Jaycees dotted the room. My fitted tux was already in my closet. All I could do was look out the window and think, "How did I get here? How is this happening?"

The first night was a welcome dinner for the winners and their spouses; we autographed hundreds of programs for the attendees the next day.

The following day, they had some business trainers of the Jaycees doing 30-minute training sessions that talked about business and communication skills, then there was lunch for everyone. It was a casual "meet and greet" for everyone. We ate, got to meet people, and answered their questions.

The night of the event, I wore my specially fitted tux. I was nervous, excited, and nearly giddy with seeing some of my childhood heroes, like Christopher Reeve. I loved him because he was strong through so much adversity, and he was someone who I could relate to. He was in his wheelchair, and I was looking forward to going up to the stage and speaking in front of him. I had no idea how badly it would go.

As I entered the ballroom, I was dazzled by the glamor of everything—nearly 4,000 people were dressed in sleek tuxedos and jewel-toned evening gowns; they milled around talking with each other as waiters and waitresses walked around with tiny hors d'oeuvres. The space was massive, about the size of two or three ballrooms combined. A huge bouquet of flowers dominated the middle at each table, with an individual rose in smaller vases dotted the plates. The linen was smooth and crisp, and I almost didn't want to use my cloth napkin because it was so fine.

The event went well at first. We ate a spectacular dinner, and as we finished, they called each award winner individually to the stage. The organizers ran a video of our story, then called us on stage, where we would accept the award and give a small speech. Then walk off. That is what was supposed to happen.

When they called my name, all I felt was excitement. I proudly rose from my table, walked with my head held high, and marched up the stairs to the stage.

That's when something changed. With each step I took across the stage, the murmur and clapping of the guests became unreasonably loud. The stage lights were so bright that I couldn't see the audience. They were also so hot that I started sweating; the back of my shirt clung to my back.

Suddenly, it became hard to breathe. I tried to shield my eyes from the lights, but I couldn't give an entire speech with one arm raised, so I tried to focus on my cards, where I had written down my speech notes.

My heart pounded.

What is going on? I thought. I had given speeches before, even to large crowds. A feeling of being utterly overwhelmed consumed me. A horrible buzzing filled my ears, and tiny dots swam at the corner of my eyes. With horror, I looked down at my notes and found that I couldn't read them. The words jiggled and danced across the paper, and my vision became blurrier.

The auditorium was now dead silent, and I realized that I hadn't said a word. Something hard lodged in my throat, and for a second, I couldn't speak. My memory went blank.

Am I having a stroke right there on stage? Am I going to die? I thought.

I gripped the podium so hard my fingers hurt. I couldn't read my notes. I couldn't even *remember* my notes. My stomach roiled with nausea.

"Th—thank you, um, for the honor," I began.

Someone coughed from the audience.

"I...um...just want to thank our wonderful sponsor, and—and—"

Flashes of my mother's face. Flashes of the knife. The boiling water. Hot dogs. Flashes of sinking into cold, unforgiving water. Sounds of metal. Sounds of a hand striking flesh.

"And thank you to the gentleman who nominated me," I finished lamely. I nodded and practically ran off the stage. I was covered in sweat. I didn't realize what was going on.

By the time I got back up to the hotel room, I was shaking. As I stood by my bed, my legs went rubbery and gave out under me. I just lost all feeling.

I had no idea what to do, so I crawled to my shower and turned the water on, soaking my clothes. I was thankful I was alone so that no one would see me. That was my first experience with severe PTSD, but I didn't know it. It would be many years before I sought the help I needed. I just lay there until the water went cold.

I Almost Started to Believe Her

I've learned over these years that words do hurt, and they do matter. I used to get slapped in the head for looking at my mom. For her, it was disrespectful and powerful to look her in the eyes. She used to tell me that my dream was too big. She often would tell me that no one in our family had done that. Who do you think you are? Followed by, "Just get a job because you're not going anywhere in life because no one else in our family has."

After 2001 and the murder of my stepdad, I was always pressed upon to never speak about it again or, "I might not be found." A direct quote from my mother's mouth. Back then, I knew that if I talked about the things I had just told millions of you, I would be dead.

After those years, many people would come forward to ask if I knew that my mom had killed *Rick*. I wasn't shocked to hear from these people or the stories they would tell me. Drugs and alcohol became a habit over the last few years of his life. It was no secret to anyone locally.

I had survived horrific child abuse as a young boy. I survived the violence of my family. I survived a car crash that should have taken my life. Now, when companies reach out to have me speak or schools, it's humbling to be open about my life and the mistakes that I have made. I can tell you I cannot share my story without mentioning God and what he did for me. None of this happened because I was lucky or had some superpower. It's always been pretty plain and simple; it was God!

Let me explain in my next part. In 2007, when Myspace was the place to be, I received a message that sent me on a new journey. Can we all take a moment to thank *Tom* for the great memories of Myspace? The message came from a young 21-year-old girl from Ohio. "Sorry to bother you, but can you look at my pics because I think we have the same dad."

I stood in my bedroom on my home computer, looking at this message for nearly thirty minutes in tears before I could even respond to her message. I couldn't believe my eyes and what I was seeing. Less than an hour after her message, I was on the phone with my dad for the first time in 30 years. I wanted to yell. I wanted to cuss at him. I wanted to ask him if he knew where he had left me and what I had gone through as a young boy. I wanted to yell and ask if he knew she had set me on fire. I raged in my mind about how I would tell him about Christmas and how if she felt I liked a toy better than my mom, she would make me take a hammer and crash my hot wheels cars. I wanted to unleash my madness on him in the first phone call, but I didn't. I just listened to him fumble his words about the weather and nonsense. A ten-minute phone call after 30 years was enough for me to feel relieved. I learned in my 50 years that it is ok to not be ok. Over the next three weeks, I had many phone calls with my dad. Finally, in September 2009, I sat down with my dad to talk about what happened and how it took place. We agreed to meet at a local Walmart at the Subway sandwich shop in *Columbus, Ohio*. For me, it was just a little over a three-hour drive. It was the longest drive of my life. I hadn't slept all night; I was scared to be another failure for my dad.

I remember pulling into that Walmart and thinking, "What was this going to do to me?" I arrived one hour early to make sure I wouldn't miss him. I wore a suit (not that $15 Goodwill suit) that day to meet my dad. I sat in my car that morning in a Walmart parking lot listening to the song *Yellow* by the music group *Coldplay*. I thought about my dad. I thought about writing this book. I want to tell him that his son gets to talk on stage with thousands of people. Mainly, I wanted to tell him how Jesus Christ saved my life. It took me many years to understand that Jesus Christ was more than a family cuss word used often in my household. I also made a phone call to a friend before I left my car. Luckily my friend answered. I ask my friend, "Should I just leave him here waiting for me, like I did him in 1979?"

He said, "The old Chad would have punched him in the face without hesitation and left. Chad, that's not who you are now." I opened my car door to head inside. I felt the Midwest fall upon my skin with every step I took. I caught a brief look at my dad walking into the Walmart. I flashback to a time when my mom told me how worthless I was and how I would end up just like my dad, broke and alone. I snapped out of this flashback to find myself sitting on a bench inside the Walmart between the automatic doors. Every time the doors opened, I saw the Subway shop inside the Walmart store. My dad sat at the first table as I watched the Walmart doors open and close. I see him sitting there looking lost, almost like he is looking for someone important.

I gathered enough courage to walk through those doors at the Columbus, Ohio, Walmart to see my dad smiling and weeping simultaneously as I shook his hand. For the first time in over 30 years, I had my dad's hand in mine. It soon became one of the most significant victories in my life at the time. My heart had forgiven. I have always heard that when one heart forgives, two hearts are healed. I felt that in my soul.

My heart cried out to help him. He seemed like an old broken man. When we spoke that day, I knew he had been through some things himself. I could see it in his brown eyes and his tears. I felt a *tsunami* of emotions. Little success that I did have, I wanted to help my dad. We walked together and talked toward the back of the store in the auto department. He said he wanted to buy new tires for his old Ford truck. My heart wanted to help him so profoundly that I purchased all the tires for his truck. I felt the guilt was shifting and not in my favor. I'm the one that felt guilty, and I was the victim back then from all those years ago. As we were walking away from paying for his tires in the auto section of Walmart, something bizarre took place, and I wouldn't know why for another month!

A lady that my dad and I did not know commented, you guys have to be father and son because you look just alike. "You should let me take a picture of you two together." We stood together in the back of Walmart with our arms around each other like we had spent the last 30 years together. The lady only told us her first name, *Grace.* That was the indication that this was God's plan all along.

Richard (my dad 2009) & Myself

Faces are sometimes different for everyone, and so are pictures. We had only been together about 1 hour before this picture of us was captured in the Walmart in Columbus, Ohio. Judging from the picture here, you would have never known we were apart for 30 years!

The drive back home was so silent, yet so loud. That three-hour drive felt like it took a lifetime. Maybe it did. As days passed, he kept his word to talk to me daily. Three weeks after our first meet-up, we were eager to meet again. This time, he would make that long three hour drive over to my house. By mid-September 2009, Indiana started to turn bitterly cold. When Dad arrived at my house, just like I knew he would, he drove up in that old Ford pickup with four new tires. We enjoyed a chuckle and walked inside.

We enjoyed a home-cooked meal that night. We talked awkwardly at times; at others, it was like best friends. As night came upon us, I suggested he stay with me for a few nights. He agreed and made his way to my couch, and I followed with pillows and a blanket. He sat there in my living room talking until late into the night. We talked about the events of that morning at that Indiana pond. My questions were short, very short. How, when, where?

He begins to tell me the entire story and what happened that summer back in the 1970s. I wasn't interested in the excuses. "I only wanted to hear the truth," I said. My dad explained the details of the summer of 1979 and what took place between him and my mother. He discussed their marriage and how violence and depression led to his departure from the family. He explained, "I had a decision to make that afternoon. Chad, I was having an affair in New York City. I would often drive my semi for work, and I met someone that was the opposite of your mother. She was kind to me. Your mother and Grandma were fuming daily, and it was impossible to live like that. Honestly, I took a load on my semi to New York City that day after I left the pond when I found out the lady I was dating was pregnant with our daughter. I never turned back and kept traveling down that highway.

I left my truck on the George Washington Bridge and walked away from everyone I loved. I even walked away from my brothers and sisters."

After the story he told me, I wanted to choke my dad. I wanted to scream. I wanted to yell; do you even know what the fuck happened to me while you were playing around? But I didn't do any of those things. The fact I didn't say a word was a *miracle*. What was happening deep in my soul was the closer that my heart and soul needed for 32 years. For all those years, I fought the voices in my head that my dad had left and was somewhere out there with millions of dollars. But, on the contrary, my dad was a broken older man now, and his wife had died. He had $32 in his bank and had run out of places to lay his head down at night.

Here we were at 10 pm on my couch, having the deepest conversation of my entire life at that point. During our conversation, I often flashed back to my incarceration in 1999 and my promise to go wherever God led me. You don't think that God will test you on those promises at that time, but he will. My goal was to travel the world to help others be less afraid. God had put me on that couch to face my dad to see if I could handle it.

So, what happens when God says yes and no? Early on, I didn't realize how that works or why it happens. It's one of those things you must grow into with faith. All I knew was I had my dad back home, and that was all that mattered to me. I had become the parent now. Sometimes the things God has asked us to follow through with are very painful. After the first week of living at my place, he finally heard me speak on stage in Indianapolis, Indiana, in front of a middle school. I saw him smile. I saw my dad taking into consideration who his son had become as a man. I watched him transform into a new man in the first three weeks together when learning about God and what he had done for me. I didn't know how God could transfer someone who was a monster at one point, and now to see this man in front was one of the most exciting things to happen to me.

During the first month together, I wanted to treat him with someone bigger than me. I took him to meet his brothers and sisters for the first time in 32 years. What an extraordinary loving moment for my dad to see all the love. I had to tell him the heartbreaking news about his mother dying. He was unaware that his mother had passed away while he was living in New York City.

Like a child, my dad asked if he could visit with them for a few days. I thought it was essential for him to try to mend the pain he caused them. I hugged everyone there. I hugged my dad, and for the first time, I said, "I love you, Pop." I drove back home those thirty miles with the biggest smile on my face. I had the windows down and the music loud.

October 15, 2009

My airplane just landed in Detroit, Michigan. I was about three hours from stepping on stage in front of 500 people when my cell phone rang. "Hello, this is Chad." On the other end of the phone was a family member on my dad's side. I was in the back seat of a cab heading to my event when my phone rang. She asks me, "Chad are you sitting down?" I replied, "Well, yes, I am. I'm in the back seat of a cab in Detroit, what's up?"

She said, "he's gone too, Chad!" "What?!" I shouted. I yelled into the phone, "Where in the hell did he go?" She said, "You don't understand. He died last night in his sleep." He had a heart attack in his sleep. I was completely disabled mentally on what was taking place. I had to be on stage in less than three more hours. I dropped the call and looked out the window. I flashed back to dad at the pond in 1979. I flashed back to the day last month I met him at the Walmart in Columbus, Ohio.

I wondered on that ride to my event what any of this meant. I ask God, why allow me to meet him and then take him away as fast as you brought him back? I only had questions without the answers to them. After my event, I flew back home to bury my dad in the town where he first started his life. I didn't understand the answer to everything that was happening until years later. He was gone for 32 years and was put back in my life for 32 days. It gave me the closure that I have always craved in my life.

His life mattered to many. His life was about life's journey and where it starts and ends. His transformation was a miracle of how fast God works. I was shown that I had to sacrifice 32 years to get 32 days with my dad. The great thing about faith is you decide whether you believe or not. But I've seen what faith can do in my life. As bad as it was, I was never alone.

That day they put my dad in the ground. I let a lot of things go. The things that hurt my heart and feelings were holding me back. They were no longer important. He made things right with everybody at the end of his life. I think that's the most important lesson of my dad: asking for forgiveness. It takes a strong man to call up everybody you have hurt to ask for forgiveness. Fortunately, in my life, I've been able to do that and receive that. It's in that magic moment that you feel God. I've never been fishing since that day at the pond in 1979 with my dad. Maybe it's time for me to take my daughter fishing.

For a few years after my dad died, I began to pull back on the things of my life. I was speaking less and less at schools. I started to feel like I always wanted to be alone. What was happening to me was about to be clear.

The Doctor

In June of 2010, I sat in a doctor's office for some relief from what was happening with my body and my thinking—two weeks before my doctor's visit. We had scheduled an MRI to see if anything was happening to my brain because of my symptoms. I wasn't sleeping at night. At all. And sometimes it was for days. Something had changed inside of me. And I didn't know what it was. I remember my doctor coming into the little room I was in then with his clipboard and pen in his right hand and his glasses on top of his head. He sat down in front of me and did some reflex checks on my legs. After he checked my blood pressure, he asked me a very important but odd question. Tell me, Chad, what was your childhood like? I looked straight down at the floor, put my hands under my legs like that 7-year-old frightened little boy again, and began to stutter. I said something that I couldn't even understand to the doctor. He patted me on the back and told me to take it easy and talk slowly. My heart felt like it was beating out of my chest. And I even began to sweat. The only thing that made sense coming out of my mouth was, "My childhood was not so good, doc."

"Chad your brain does show something that I want to make you aware of." This frightened me so badly that I wanted to run out of his office and into traffic. You know one of those times where everything comes to your mind at once?

"Chad, you have PTSD. That's what's causing all of this to you. It's from the trauma you have been through throughout your life. You're probably not going to be able to work anymore." He went on to tell me that PTSD was a brain damage injury caused by the trauma. He asked me a series of questions that morning. Have you ever been in a grocery store and found yourself lost? Have you ever heard a song on the radio that brings you back to the 1980s? Does your mom show up in your dreams at night?

I thought, "Many odd questions Doc." I answered every one of them that he had for me. All my answers pointed directly to five letters. C-PTSD. I began the long journey to learn and educate myself on what C-PTSD was and what the triggers would be for me.

The things I discovered about the injury to the brain were like they were the ones writing my life story and not me. Every word I discovered from my studies on PTSD was so much like what I was going through. I had daytime flashbacks of the trauma and heard my mother's voice everywhere I went telling me, "I'm going to f@%kin kill you!" At night I had horrific nightmares of my mother stabbing me repeatedly. By 2012, I was tired of this torment to my body and mentally.

The thing is, we carry trauma in our bodies. Even if we don't think about it on a day-to-day basis, our body keeps a record of all that has happened to us. We need to take breaks, to rest, or otherwise, our bodies will force us to.

That's what happened to me—I had a stroke that left me unable to walk or speak for a year. My body gave up fighting for a while, forcing me to rest and recuperate.

I needed a break from myself. I needed a restart. I remembered a film that I watched a few years back. The movie inspired my life to start where I was. The movie, *The Pursuit of Happiness*, was released with a budget of $55 million. As the movie played on my DVD player, watching it would forever change my life.

By now, all my speaking engagements had dried up, and I was nearly broke. It was my last chance to get back up.

I stayed in a nursing home for about a year. Once again, I had the sense of being the odd man out. At 38, I was one of the youngest people there. I had to go to physical and speech therapy until I learned to walk and talk again.

It was not easy. Part of me wanted to give up. I had suffered so many blows in life that I thought that maybe I would die soon. Nursing homes are depressing by nature—they smell like antiseptic and old age, and so many people who live there are lonely. I couldn't do anything for myself for a while; I could only communicate through writing in a little notebook.

However, a movie would change my life. A few weeks into my stay, a pastor visited the nursing home, a DVD tucked under one arm and a warm smile on his face. He came every so often with different movies to lift the residents' spirits and talk and listen to them.

When he saw me, he was slightly dumbfounded.

"You're so young," he said. "What are you doing here?"

I scribbled a word on my notepad: Stroke.

Maybe he could see something in my eyes, some vitality left. He believed in me when I didn't even believe in myself.

"Come on," he said. "I think this movie will help you."

At first, I was skeptical. How could a movie help me? I had to have nurses lift and bathe me, and I couldn't speak. But I attended the movie showing since there was nothing else to do.

The opening credits of *The Pursuit of Happiness* flickered to life on my TV screen. As I watched Will Smith transform into the real life of Christopher Gardner from San Francisco, California, my mindset began to transform. My thoughts from my life became clear in my head.

If he can do it, so can I, I thought. Here was a man who chased after opportunity like his life depended on it, and it did not only for him but for his son. So I thought if Christopher Gardner could make his life dream come true while caring for a 5-year-old son, then I could.

As the movie went on, something profound shifted inside of me. I was going to make it, no matter what. No matter what happened or what obstacles I faced, I would pursue my dream.

I didn't even know what that dream was, except it was anything but staying in a nursing home for the rest of my life.

I looked around me. I was tucked into cheap sheets, staring at bland, beige walls with nothing more for entertainment or mental stimulation than a TV.

I can stay here and grow old, I thought. Or I can pursue my happiness.

Making that choice was easy, but sticking to it would prove to be one of the hardest things I've done. But there was still some temptation to remain where I was. As humans, we want to stay with what is familiar and comfortable. The unknown is scary; many people never trust themselves enough to take a chance.

That movie forced me to look at my life thus far. So many times, I could have died. So many times of getting shot, sinking into water, or even attempting to take my own life; even the stroke was a brush with death too close for comfort.

What if I stayed alive for a reason? I thought.

I didn't know what that reason was yet. I just knew that I had to get out of the nursing home.

I promised myself that *I would make it, no matter what.*

By the end of the movie, a single driving force had unified itself in my mind. If Chris Gardner could find opportunities in the 80s without the technology that we have now, then I could.

Through a verbal agreement with the pastor, he promised that if I learned to walk again and get back on my feet, he would purchase a one-way ticket to San Francisco.

So that's what happened. I took the first steps toward healing. I worked harder at physical and speech therapy. Eventually, the pastor fulfilled his end of our bargain.

After purchasing a one-way bus ticket from Fort Wayne, Indiana, to San Francisco, California, it left me with just $8.34 to my name. I traveled halfway across the United States on a Greyhound bus heading to the west coast. I only carried a backpack. By the third day on the bus, I began to think I was making a huge mistake. I was so hungry. I began to hear voices telling me to give up and go back home. I said to myself, you can't go back there. You only have a one-way ticket. I knew in the beginning to buy a one-way ticket because sometimes it doesn't want us to go back to a few places that once hurt us. I bought some saltine crackers for 99 cents which left me with a little over $7. One of many things I wasn't prepared for was how cold it would be in San Francisco when I arrived at 8:00 pm.

I stepped off the bus and a sense of wilderness and hunger. I had $7.18 in my pocket. I had two changes of clothes. I had one zip-up sweatshirt, and I was wearing a pair of shorts. I had a dream: to start my whole life over and take my story to a bigger vision than what I could see. The Bay Bridge was one of the first images I saw when I stepped off that Greyhound bus. I'd never seen the Bay Bridge in my entire life. What a beautiful sight I was looking at. I was cold and hungry. These eyes have never seen that much beauty in a bridge. The bridge connected San Francisco to Oakland, CA.

The Bay Bridge, San Francisco, California

The only thing I could do then was walk toward the Bay Bridge and hope to find something to eat with the little I had left in my pocket. I found myself walking down *Embarcadero Ave* in San Francisco. It was very cold as temperatures back home surged. However, in San Francisco, the temperatures were much cooler year-round. I had no clue what I was getting myself into. I had no job, nowhere to sleep, and I didn't know one single person in the city or even in the whole state!

So, I did what I do best, I walked. I walked toward the water. I was looking for what I was here for. I knew only two things at that time. One, I only had $7.18, and I was broken as hell. The second thing I realized that evening was I knew I wouldn't be one day! I had a dream and would die before giving up on it. The bitter winds from the bay were cutting through me like a table saw. I figured it was California; it's supposed to be hot right? Well, certainly not for the San Francisco Bay area. It was much cooler than the Los Angeles area.

I was not prepared for that type of weather with the clothes I had on. With every step I took, I had hunger pains from not eating for three days on the bus. I had traveled over 1,500 miles to get here. Before I knew it, I was walking under the famous Bay Bridge. I felt like I was dreaming. I wanted to come here since I was seven years old. I saw it on our TV back home, and here I was. The *Kewanna kid* had made the journey. Most of my friends said I was crazy or would die on the streets. Not even one had been to San Francisco or took a risk like this. It wasn't long before I found myself on Pier 39. That's the place where my voyage started. Friends I had known for 20-plus years said I was just a pretender and crazy. I wasn't doing this to impress them or anyone else. I knew my dream was here, but I didn't know where.

Pier 39, San Francisco, California 2012

The first thing I heard was Christmas music coming from the speakers. It made me feel like a little boy again. The little shops and restaurants were like a *mini-Walt Disney* to me that I see on TV.

Everything was so picturesque; it was like I had been dropped on the set of a movie about fishermen. The hardwood deck under my feet was slippery with mist that constantly rose from the sea. The air was thick with the scent of salt and ocean brine, and the wind whipped my face and tugged at my clothes. Families with their children, tourists, and couples strolled along the docks. I passed a massive staircase shaped like piano keys, then a brightly lit carousel, where kids yelled in delight. The smell of frying fish drifted over everything, and seagulls squawked overhead. The gentle lap of water against the docks was comforting. Restaurants and bars beckoned with large windows, and my stomach rumbled. I was getting my bearings but needed to learn how to make money.

Street performers lined up to entertain the crowds for tips. I heard a man on a microphone talking about his show that he would put on in 10 minutes. I waited around to see his juggling show on stage at Pier 39. It wasn't like I had any place to go.

At the end of his show, people would walk up to his bucket to tip him. On the second level, restaurants were closing for the night. I probably watched two hundred people leave a famous restaurant from upstairs.

They put my wheels in motion. I needed cash as soon as possible, or I wouldn't make it here.

I decided to work as a server to make the cash I needed immediately. All I had to do was get a manager to view my jump drive in my pocket, and I would get hired. So that's what I did.

I walked into that restaurant like I owned it, with only $7.18 in my pocket. I exuded a confidence I didn't feel but had nothing to lose. I remember taking that escalator to the top of Pier 39 to the second level. Every second that passed, I thought, am I crazy for doing what I have done?? I mean, there was no way back. I burnt all my bridges and got a one-way ticket. I had to make it. I didn't have any excuses left or anyone to turn to. Any success or failure would now be all me, all my responsibility.

I walked into the first restaurant that looked nice enough that dinners would probably give good tips.

The hostess cheerfully greeted me and asked if I was dining alone or with a group.

"Actually, I'm wondering if you're doing any hiring?"

She shook her head, her mouth forming a sad smile, and said, "I'm sorry, we're not."

I put my head down and looked at the ground like that scared 7-year-old boy in front of my mother. Even though I knew logically that the first place I went to probably wouldn't hire me, the rejection stung nonetheless.

I turned to walk out, and a gentleman approached me. His name plate said that he was the manager. He wore all black and a sharp, satin red tie.

"Sir, is there anything I can help you with?"

Here's my chance.

Sometimes, opportunities come at the smallest moments, but you have to recognize them. I hoped that seeing the manager was some kind of sign; I had not been pushy or demanded to see the manager, but he had appeared nonetheless.

I said, "I was just stopping in to see if you were doing any hiring."

Please hire me. Please hire me.

Even though my heart raced with hope, I tried to appear as calm and casual as possible, like I wasn't desperate—which I was.

He replied, "What are you looking to do? We might have a dishwasher spot open."

"Well, actually, I was hoping to apply to be a server because I'm good with people."

He nodded. "Do you have a resume or any experience?"

It was like seeing light at the end of the tunnel. I had to refrain from *laughing out loud* at his question.

I told him, "If you go into your office and open this jump drive, I guarantee you will hire me right now."

His eyebrows raised in surprise. "Oh really? What's your name?"

"Chad Gaines."

"Well, Mr. Gaines, let's take a look."

A few minutes later, I found myself walking up the steps to his office. With every step, my heart hammered in my throat. I just knew that he would hire me once he saw my experience as a public speaker. Still, that tiny voice of doubt crept in. What if he didn't? What if they didn't have any room for any more hires?

He pushed my jump drive into his computer. He clicked on a few files and listened to me speak. For a moment, I was afraid that I had overstepped, that maybe I had been too confident or overestimated myself.

And then his eyes lit up.

He instantly turned to me and said, "How many hours a week are you looking for?"

"As many as I'm allowed to work in San Francisco."

Without filling out an application, he hired me right on the spot. "Welcome to the team, Mr. Gaines," he said, shaking my hand. "I've got to say that I'm curious." He gestured to the jump drive, took it out, and handed it back to me. "With experience like that, how come you want to work here?"

I grinned sheepishly. "Well, public speaking isn't exactly stable. Opportunities come and go. I came out here to San Francisco so I could start over. I needed a fresh place, somewhere new." I also had some confessing to do. I added, "Also, I just got here on a bus less than two hours ago. I have no money or food or a place to sleep. Do you know where I could go?"

The manager took my words in stride, as if homeless public speakers appeared on his doorstep daily. "Well, the good thing is you now work at a restaurant. I'll make sure you eat every single day that you work. Unfortunately, I can't help you out with a place to live or stay because of our policies, but I can tell you the nearest place to go to get something to eat with the money you have."

I thanked him, and the weight of not having a job finally lifted from my chest. I could breathe easier knowing that I would have a regular income to rely on.

"Just show up ready to work on Monday," he said.

I promised I would, then walked less than a mile to a burger joint. I swear, that was the best burger of my life after not eating for three days. I was relieved I had a job and food in my belly within two hours of pulling into San Francisco. However, I still had not found a warm place to sleep.

Soon I discovered that my journey was about how badly I wanted success and not so much about the little things, like where to sleep. I wandered around Fisherman's Wharf until late into the night, trying to figure out my next move. Eventually, I would find my home for the next 1,000 cold nights. It was the steps of 505 Beach Street. Just far enough away from the cold breeze of the bay but close enough to walk to work the next morning and every day after. I know my journey could have ended there, and I wanted so badly to give up. I learned about the streets and that lifestyle as I moved forward.

I realized that my body at 39 was not as forgiving as it was at 29. I woke up the next morning on those steps around 5:00 am and walked to Starbucks to shave in their bathroom and prepare for my first day of work. Every inch of my body hurt from the pain of sleeping on those steps. I found myself dozing off in the chair of Starbucks. My first day of work went well. So many things to learn, and my goal was to learn and be more productive than anyone in the building. It took time because I didn't want anyone to know what I was going through then. Soon days turned into weeks. It was about one week from the Christmas holiday. Business picked up like I'd never seen before in my 39 years. My life had been saved for a bigger purpose. I know that must sound cliche or whatever topic you may label it. But it was true, and I felt a bigger purpose existed for me creeping in. I just needed to *stay focused* at my job and outwork myself day after day.

I stayed with the same routine because one thing I learned the hard way was with PTSD; routine is and was everything. It helps on the bad days. At that time, I was making more money in one week than I used to make in one month! I had made $3,000 in two weeks of work! I had to decide on a few things that would crush my dream or take me to the next level.

I found my calling. It wasn't about the job; it was about the people. If I knew one thing in my life, it was people. That first year, I slept on the streets 365 nights and worked most of that year six days a week. At the end of my first year, I made $92,000. In my years here on earth, I have discovered that blocking out everything that society says you need can make you a fortune. I didn't have a home, and I didn't have a car payment, no utilities to pay either. I wouldn't suggest this journey to anyone. I cried many nights in the cold, knowing I had to work in the morning. My body hurt to the point that it was unbearable on my bones. I soon found myself trying to decide whether to continue to sleep on the steps of 505 beach street or spend my money on the hefty rent of San Francisco. My dream was bigger than some apartment on Powell Street.

I knew this journey would not be easy. I knew it was going to hurt when I stepped off that bus. My goal was to be better than I was yesterday at work. I kept my head down and focused. It was almost in a blink of an eye that three years had passed. I spent over 1,500 nights on the streets of San Francisco. I had seen things I never thought I would see. I saw people smoking meth in the open and on the sidewalks. I saw a man walking out of the grocery store and getting stabbed and robbed for $31 worth of food.

By my third year at work, I had saved $83,000 cash. My street smarts were paying off in a big way. I walked the streets some nights until my bones hurt. I always thought about how to improve and faster at my job. I studied and studied to be better and to do better. On other nights, my mind drifted while I lay on the cardboard with my *two blankets*. Can a guy from Kewanna, Indiana, with $7 in his pocket, make out in the big city? I talked to God every night.

He had shown me so much grace. Whether you believe in him or not. I managed to turn my $7 into $83,000. For me, that was a huge deal.

I was able to bless so many on my journey. Giving was everything. I gave away $50,000 of cash while sleeping on the streets. It warmed my heart to see so many smiles. I did it with nothing more than a backpack and a hungry heart. Most nights, I heard my mother's voice telling me to give up and go back home. Home, I thought? What the hell was home? What was a family?

Everyone Talks to God

I flashback, and I remember mixing all the pop fountain drinks as a kid and thinking I was such a rebel. 1980 was such an innocent time in America.

It's 1981, and I'm waiting for this show to come on the radio. I love his radio voice and his long-distance dedication letter and song. This is Casey Kasem's American Top 40. These are the type of flashbacks I would often have.

A phone call came through my messenger on Facebook. It came after nearly ten years of not talking to my cousin. His message on social media came as a surprise.

"Chad, call me back!"

I can only remember saying hello. After that, the conversation took on a forum of itself. He called to tell me my mom had just days to live.

Evidently, the doctors found an aneurysm. She had already had brain surgery, and there was nothing more they could do. The hospice team was getting called in. On April 10, 2017, my mother was pronounced dead in the nursing home she shared with my grandmother. Three doorways away was my grandmother, slowly dying from breast cancer and Alzheimer's disease. My mind often wondered, while being homeless to working all the time, did my mother talk to God before she passed? Just as she had wished, there was no mention of me in her obituary.

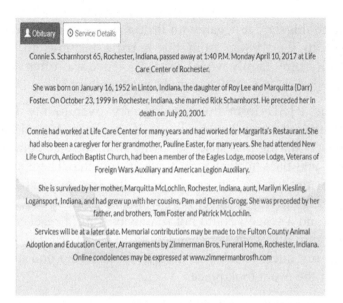

Connie Foster Scharnhorst was cremated and put in a plot next to my stepdad, who she had murdered in 2001. The idea that never sits too easy with me.

Cause of Death:

Five months after my mother's death, my grandmother, Marquitta McLochlin, was pronounced dead at the same nursing home from Alzheimer's disease.

A psychiatrist once asked me, "When your mother dies, and you don't get the closure you need, how is that going to make you feel?" I didn't know how to respond at that point, and I didn't know how to respond on April 10th, 2017.

I think it was made easier by my dad because I got the closure I felt I needed. With my mother, there was no peace or letting go. It became a revolving door of thoughts and nightmares that continue to this day. It began with little flashbacks of episodes that happened in the 1980s, from the horrific beatings to the odd conversations my family would have. Violence was often practiced during the holidays as well as family get-togethers.

The PTSD from this would carry over to my finances, relationships, and how I viewed myself as a man. I would always catch myself staring into space far away from the city lights of San Francisco and back to that farm town in Indiana. There's nothing easy about my trip to San Francisco in the first place. I lost both parents along the way. I had closure from one of them; the other was a thought and a voice I could not run away from. I reached out for help to figure out what was happening to me. I learned so many things on my quest to educate myself about PTSD and its effects years after the event took place.

I don't know much about anything. I can tell you, however, quite a story. I can tell you what it's like to jump from 2 stories off a boat into the Pacific Ocean off the coast of Honolulu. I can tell you what it's like to walk into a movie set and the excitement that comes with it. I can also tell you what feeling small and less than zero is like. All of life, we will encounter grief, shortcomings, heartbreak, and some small victories in between.

People always ask me, "How did you know you had PTSD?" In the beginning, I had no clue. I didn't know what PTSD even was. It took over three years of testing to figure out the cause of all this. Within those three years, they treated my symptoms and did not relate them to one cause. First, I was tested for ALS or Lou Gehrig's disease, where they stick needles into your muscles and track the muscle movements to your brain. Everything came back clear from that test. A week after that, I was tested for Parkinson's disease, and I had to walk a straight line in the doctor's office. He used some fancy devices to check my reflexes. And then, I was taken into another room where I was put on a table, and they inserted a needle into my spine to withdraw fluid and check for Parkinson's disease. Once again, everything came back clear. We were almost at a stopping point during a 2018 doctor's visit. After an MRI showed four white spots on my brain, it had the characteristics of 2 different diagnoses. One was the cause of the memory loss, and the other part of the brain showed a sign of PTSD. After answering a series of questions from my doctor, he asked me one final question. "Chad, what was your childhood like?" Finally, after three years of testing, we had an answer. And he spoke the words, "You have PTSD."

There is no cure for PTSD. There are, however, many coping skills to get through the rest of your life. It's something the imagination cannot touch. Even though the diagnosis was grim and life expectancy is 20 years shorter than the average person, I was just relieved we had a name to go with all these symptoms.

It's called life, and we can't get out of it alive. Somewhere between 2018 and 2019, I caught myself writing down simple drink orders, and I would forget the order within the 50 seconds it took me to get to the soda machine. As time progressed, I would lose my balance and run into tables, leading to big leg bruises. By the spring of 2019, I would forget the lines of a book I was reading. Even with people I worked with daily for a few years, I would lose their names somewhere in my brain. I would spend many hours focusing on reading name tags to remember some of my friends.

Even so much as leaving my keys in my P.O. Box at the post office more than eight times. I would dismiss it as I'm just getting older, I guess. My brain wouldn't process conversations I would have with my guests at work.

For me, I believe 2020 opened the floodgates to how this was affecting my mental health. After being laid off from COVID, I became isolated from nearly everyone. I didn't want to go out or talk to people. I didn't know how to explain it, how I was a public speaker, but that light was losing its brightness.

I listened to music for about 14 hours daily to fight off what I heard in my head. I wasn't sleeping at night. I would only sleep when it became daylight outside my window. I made 12 trips across the country and back that year; I could barely tell you about 3 of them. Again, none of this was easy for 40 years of my life. I carried the blame for being unable to make my mom and dad feel better about their inner self.

The physical abuse became so standard in my home that I thought it was unusual for other kids in my school not to get hit by their parents. As time passed, my widespread bruises and other markings healed on my body. However, the emotional abuse that I consistently suffered in the disrobing of my youth was more difficult to define.

My emotional abuse began in my home when I was around *seven years old*, with continual teasing for wetting the bed and belittling that always led to verbal attacks and out-of-control physical abuse. I have learned so much in my forty-one years of breath here. I know great people were put in my life, and if I had ignored any of them, I wouldn't be doing what I do now.

God has given me more than one chance. The critics would play it off as I'm lucky, I'm crazy, or I don't play by the rules. Well, knowing where I was in life and where I am today, I would say they are right in a big part. However, my life has never been about getting knocked down; it's about Getting Back Up.

I have just humbled myself on these pages of this book you now hold in your hands. You also have two choices now. You can close it and pile it under a bunch of papers on your kitchen table and forget my name, or if you would like to help me open up this case and the truth of what happened to my stepdad. I encourage you all to ask questions. I encourage you all to make phone calls, send emails, make videos–whatever it takes to make this wrong, right.

Indiana 1984

I'm sitting in our living room on our yellow shag carpet. I'm playing with my hot-wheel cars. My mom still hasn't come home from work. I never know which mom is going to come home from work. Would it be the pretend-smiling mother or the raging out-of-control abusive mom? This time I was punished for not doing the dishes before my mother got home from work. I reflect on this turning point because of a couple of different things. One was the fact that I cherish those hot-wheel cars so much. This time my mother took my blue hot wheels car, which was my favorite one, and smashed it with a hammer until there was nothing left but a flat piece of metal. Those mental and emotional games continued for most of her life until she died in 2017. My phone calls to her went unanswered, and so did my chance of getting any closure. Since I was the only child between my parents and most of my family was now gone, I returned to life's basics. During my 5th year of working and three years on the streets, I made just a little bit of money to invest in a couple of companies. That changed my mindset, and I would eventually find people who see more in me than I see in myself.

My mindset shifted back to business and the people I could learn from. I started to meet people again from all over the country. I met bankers, I met CEOs of companies, and I met award-winning authors that helped me every step of the way. In 1984, I was 11 years old. It was one of the biggest turning points in my life. The 1980s culture and music would stay with me for the rest of my life. However, those memories of what took place in my life would also haunt me forever.

This book could be a life manual for many of you, including my daughter. One day she will find her journey outside the home, and I want her to be prepared for what's out there. No one teaches us about the real world, and I think that's the most important thing I need to equip her with – the challenges outside the home. The outside world is much different than it was in 1984.

In 1984, my grandfather could give me a note, and I could confidently walk into a grocery store and buy him a pack of cigarettes. So much has changed since then between people, cultures, income, and personalities. I have personally seen the human will to live is the most incredible thing on the planet. I've seen people that started with nothing become something. It's just a matter of how bad you want it. There is a great lesson that I have learned from author Christopher Gardner. His mindset is to start where you are with what you have. Those are the same principles I talk and coach about throughout my journey worldwide. I've seen so many talented people that had absolutely nothing, build something that the world can use. One of the very few things that I believe PTSD cannot touch is the imagination to dream.

One of my mentors asked me to write down my goals for this book. Whether it would be where I travel with it, how many people I can make smile from it, or how many sales I can generate from it. At the time, I had very few answers to those questions. I was always mentally programmed to believe that if you were born poor, you would stay poor. If you lived in this area, that's where you would stay until the day you die. We are programmed to believe in negative thoughts from negative people. I began to take notes about my own life on everything that transpired up until I was at the point where I was ready to get up on stage and share my life story. Even though I was no longer that little boy, I carried him inside of me and probably always will. I found myself trying to protect him from the voices in my head that my mother had placed there over 40 years ago. As years passed and I grew as a man, I learned to ignore them and not give them power. I realized with a lot of therapy that they would never go away. I had to accept who I was then and who I am now.

A few symptoms I have personally suffered from include: flashbacks throughout the day, mood changes from one hour to the next, feeling on edge, and being very aware of my surroundings. At restaurants, I tend to overhear conversations three tables away because of hyper-awareness caused by PTSD. In my research, I have found PTSD also has a lot of different symptoms, 25 in total. PTSD feels different for everyone. This is partly because the trauma affects each individual experience. Substance abuse is normally one of the symptoms to cover up the pain. I've also found another symptom of mine: wetting the bed until 9 years old. I experience very graphic nightmares. Later in my life, I've become less interested in activities and people. Depression is a big part of the problem regarding this brain injury. I wake up depressed every day--not about one thing, but about a thousand things. You almost must trick the brain into believing positive thoughts just so you can get through the day. Some days it feels like a heavy boulder in a backpack on your back. Nothing can be done or said to make a person feel happy.

Another symptom is blaming yourself or others for what the abuser did to you. I often have trouble concentrating. I have short-term memory loss. I'm easily startled by certain loud noises. I twitch in my sleep quite often from nightmares that I'm fighting. Throughout all these symptoms I've been experiencing, I have found the most important thing to me is routine. My wife Tina is my biggest fan. She is the most patient person that I know. That is a significant part of healing from PTSD, to have a robust support system in your home.

I would describe life just like football. It's all about blocking and tackling. You must block distractions and tackle the opportunities. These skills can be applied to anyone's life. It's an ongoing process that must be yours. College students always ask me, "What is the best advice you can give us?" I would undoubtedly say the most significant gift I can give you is "Life is going to hurt you!" I give them the hard truth because they deserve to hear the truth.

Life will uppercut you in your mouth. Life will kick you when you're already down and hurting. Life will jab you in the nose many times along the way. It's a fight, I tell them. We can't always be soft with our children. Life is hard, and it should be explained. If I didn't learn anything from my failures throughout my life, I might not be doing what I'm doing now. We often learn more from our failures than our successes. Is there anyone here looking back at their past mistakes who does not wish they would have done the good and wholesome thing instead of the unproductive one? I tried to remember my failures from my past when I'm on the road, traveling our country, speaking to thousands of people that demand my help. It's exhausting at times. It's lonely and takes time away from my family back home. I learned life is about choices; we all have the same 24 hours in the day. I often perform an autopsy, so to speak, on my own mistakes.

No one on earth is harder on Chad Gaines than Chad Gaines himself. Sometimes that's what's best for me. Other times, it holds me back from the work I must do at home and on the road. I always ask myself about once a week, what was the tipping point in my life? I've always attempted to understand where I passed the point of no return. Was it my mom's abuse of me? Was it the drugs and alcohol I put in my body that should have killed me four times over? Was it losing my best friend at the age of 18? Was it the horrific car wreck that I was able to walk away from? I certainly believe it was a little bit of everything. Steve Jobs once said, "You can only put the pieces together by looking back at your life."

I've seen enough anguish in our schools nationwide to convince me that evil is real and death is a regular and frequent intruder on humanity.

Remember that first suit I bought for $15? I wore that for the first year of speaking and made over $40,000 in that $15 suit. So don't pretend to be clueless or think you can't do something extraordinary in your life with what you have. I've learned to surround myself with people that are growing and not just in height. Again, not an easy thing to do overnight. For my first thirty years, I carried the blame for being unable to make my mother and dad feel better about their inner self. To me, friends, this is what discovery and recovery are all about! Letting go and letting God handle the messy stuff we don't always discuss. Reflecting on my childhood, I can see how emotionally deprived I was when I was a young boy and a teenager.

Please don't ignore whatever you are called to do on this planet. Our time here is short, as you have read about my experiences. We are simply renting space for a moment. As a man and a father of a 7-year-old, I can honestly say I believe in you. Every one of you! If I can do what I did with absolutely nothing, then certainly, with all your talent and beauty, you can change a part of the world. If you are wrestling with life's trials, I hope my words empower you to want to do more in your life and celebrate your victories. Who better to offer comfort and understanding in times of your trials or grief than someone who has already been through a similar experience? When you're suffering, would you rather talk to somebody who can speak only about what they heard? And agree with you? Or would you rather surround yourself with people who already walked a mile in your shoes?

How cool is that a little boy from Kewanna, Indiana, would end up where I am right now in my life! I have a beautiful and loving wife that supports me every step of the way. I have a 7-year-old daughter who keeps me accountable for things I say and promise others. This is my team. This is my story. I am a warrior.

In 2020, I met the writer who wrote the "Sons of Anarchy" series. I had the pleasure of sitting down with him to discuss the possibility of writing my life story for the big screen. That's when I finally realized this story was much bigger than I was. I didn't set out to write my story for fame or a multi-million-dollar deal. I wanted to write my story to help people who suffer from this brain injury and have no resources or communication to talk about how they feel. I realized God was using that little boy to start a movement. A movement to talk about mental health and not be embarrassed or ashamed about it. After a lengthy discussion with the Hollywood writer, I decided to move forward with the screenplay based on my life. And those are just some of the few things that helped change my life in so many ways. I really believe in the phrase, "Never give up on your dreams no matter the obstacles in front of you." I want this book and movie to be an open platform for people to speak out about the tragedies in life and the victories. You don't have to be ashamed of where you come from. But also understand you don't have to stay there either. So many great people have influenced, educated, and given me small amounts of knowledge to get me to the next place in my life. That probably started in 1980, with learning how to grow a garden and the fundamentals of what family was really like through Margaret and Bob Davis.

Many people often ask, "Why do you think God lets things happen like this?" It was a long quest for me to answer that question. I think I always wanted to understand that myself. And I think this is how things work. When you pray for strength, I believe God gives you hard obstacles to overcome so you can grow and have the strength you pray for. When I prayed for knowledge, He gave me problems to figure out. Now, I want to ask you some things so you can think about this on your own, "At what point in your life did God ask you to get out of the boat, and you resisted?" I also want you to think about who talked you out of your dreams so you gave up and settled for what you have and where you are.

If people understood how precious life is, they would be in the streets, high-fiving and hugging each other daily instead of hiding behind a keyboard and disrespecting each other on social media. We never know when we will have that last conversation with a best friend or relative. The only thing I had in mind when writing this book was to make people less afraid. I wanted to give them something they could relate to. I've come across people that want to speak out, and I've also come across those who refuse to talk about their own stories for various reasons.

I want to give you a few nuggets that helped me, and maybe somewhere down the road, it can help you. It took me many years to understand that this was not my fault. Yes, my mom beat the shit out of me. Yes, she kicked me in the face and broke my nose. Yes, she stabbed me with a butcher knife and even set me on fire. But in her mind, she loved me. But the truth of the matter was, she feared me. She feared the fact that I would escape that misery, that atmosphere, that culture, and that family and talk to you about what happened. For me, I have reached the biggest goal in my life. A peaceful home that I share with my wife. A seven-year-old daughter that often asks about her grandparents, a challenge that I still face as I write this sentence to you right now. There are so many meanings of life and purposes of life that people don't understand. Mental health is a huge problem that needs to be addressed in the United States and many other countries. My quest will take me around the world, not sharing my story but sharing other people's stories of how they are healing from PTSD.

Daily Life

Movies and TV shows frequently use flashbacks to demonstrate the challenges of a character suffering from PTSD. From Chris Lyle's flashback-fueled meltdowns in American Sniper to Charlie's emotional memories in The Perks of Being a Wallflower, flashbacks are often the first symptom to come to mind when people discuss PTSD. I find this to be very true in my own life.

I first started getting PTSD and body memory flashbacks when I was in middle school. Because my trauma lasted so long, my flashbacks have been unique and unforgiving. I don't have a single, full-picture memory that plays out in my head as you see in movies. I experience specific memories this way, but many of my traumatic memories are tucked away in my mind and hidden from the surface. Like many victims of *child abuse,* I have trouble remembering the details of my 30s and most of my 40s years.

Since there are a lot of holes in my adulthood memories, I experience my flashbacks through body memories instead. Body memories can be described as somatic memories expressed through physiological changes to the body. It simply means my body feels what it was feeling during the traumatic event. It feels heavy and executes physical pain in different areas of my body throughout the days and nights.

It differs depending on the trigger, but my flashback body memories usually start with a hot flash the first minute I open my eyes in the morning. After that, my body begins to sweat, my heart picks up speed, and small noises around me grow louder and louder. I get this sick feeling in my *stomach* similar to nausea but better described as the feeling of pure panic, like waking up and realizing you slept through an exam. My triggers for a body memory flashback can be anything from an angry tone of voice to the sound of a punching bag being hit at my gym.

For a long time, I wasn't aware that I was experiencing body memories. The feelings I get during these flashbacks are similar to the ones I get during a panic attack. It was, and is, hard to distinguish the two symptoms from each other. However, my therapist eventually helped me see the connection, and understanding my body memory flashbacks helped me understand my trauma better.

Strangely, body memories help validate what I went through. The way I feel during a flashback is the same way I felt as a young boy trapped in a violent household with *no way to escape.* Remembering how I felt during my childhood helps me have empathy toward myself and respect for my healing journey. It's not easy on most days. Dealing with body memory flashbacks in the present can be difficult. The best way to cope so far is to give myself space. My trauma happened at the hands of other people, so getting away from people is the first thing I do when I start to feel an episode happening. Going somewhere quiet and cool to let the body's memory pass helps me calm down faster.

Everybody experiences flashbacks differently, and how you cope with yours will be unique to you. While they can be painful reminders of your trauma, learning how to live with them is possible. Pay attention to how you feel during a flashback and give yourself what you need during that moment. Above all, be compassionate towards yourself. *Self-love* and self-acceptance are the first steps toward a peaceful life. Have you experienced body memory flashbacks? What do they feel like to you?

My PTSD nightmares, however, have stuck with me. They're the one symptom of PTSD I can't figure out. No amount of medication or therapy I have had, I have never been able to erase what my mind sees when I fall asleep.

Because I lived through continuous trauma over my childhood, I don't have typical recurring nightmares. Rather than repeatedly replaying the same traumatic event, my dreams fall into recurring categories. It can vary depending on what's happening in my day-to-day life, but my nightmares most commonly involve themes of death, pain, and fear seven nights a week.

For example, I once dreamed I was getting eaten alive by my Mother. In the dream, my friends stood by and watched as my

Mother consumed me piece by piece with a steak knife. This particular nightmare wasn't a replay of a past event, as nothing like that happened in my real life (and I'm confident my friends would help me escape). Instead, the dream encompassed the fear and helplessness I felt growing up, with everyone watching my pain but no one stepping in to help.

When I first started getting nightmares, I tried to avoid them. Lacking proper prescriptions then, I would take over-the-counter medications that made me drowsy to fall asleep. Or, on bad days, I would stock up on candy bars and sodas with the hopes of avoiding sleep entirely. The nightmares have continued for about 40 years.

While my nightmares bothered me at the start of my PTSD recovery, I've grown to appreciate them. They can be very unpleasant, but I've found that they are a way for my mind to process the deep traumas and fear I am unable or unwilling to face during the day. In a strange way, they provide a place for my brain to work through memories and feelings bothering me on a level I'm not ready to face yet. That said, I have trouble with my feelings and confusion nearly every day on this journey.

The facts are evident across the board regarding dating or marrying someone with a PTSD brain injury. If they tell you the truth like I'm about to, the facts are you have a 90% chance of relationship problems or failure in the first six months. That's the bad news first.

There are many factors involved when dating with PTSD. I have failed in 100% of my relationships. That statement is very true. My thoughts were always weighed down by trust issues and visions of things that never happened in my relationships. I would physically get exhausted trying to prove something in my relationships that were simply never there. I didn't have the adult skills to ever discover a safe relationship. It took five decades to figure that out. Even at fifty years old, I'm learning things like the new guy at work. Learning is a big part of the PTSD journey for me.

In my life, I was probably suffering the effects of PTSD early in my childhood. The first two people in my life that were supposed to protect me (My Mother and Dad) did not do so. The effects of that carried into my adulthood relationships. As a man, I became filled with bitterness and jealousy in my adult relationships. I was always looking for that long-term marriage, but my brain always said, "Run!" Running away from things and people is common in people with PTSD. The PTSD brain is triggered when it gets scared. Trust becomes so lost in the middle of an argument that it triggers the brain to run away.

It has taken me years to learn the techniques to remain silent and listen during a heated conversation. The triggers I face today in my 50s are not the triggers I faced in my 20s and so on. Life changes, and so do triggers dealing with PTSD.

I have, since the age of twenty-six years old, had the overwhelming feeling in my life that just maybe God wants us to meet a few wrong people before meeting the right one so that when we finally meet the right person, we will know how to be grateful for that gift. Some even say we are being taught lessons every day.

Some are open to learning but wait for the teacher to attend. Some don't realize when the teacher shows up for the teaching. At the age of twenty-six, I was living in the latter. I have learned a great deal while on that journey and the journey I now follow with God. Courage is not about standing still in one place for very long; it is about doing things no one else will do because fear or embarrassment stops them.

In the very beginning, I feared writing my story for many years. I've been in danger from threats. I can no longer be afraid of them. In this world we now live in, you can't be afraid to get yourself embarrassed. I sat on the upper deck of a church of more than 3,000 for the first time. I sat alone, wondering if this was even real. I'm broken, lonely, and mad, and the current events in my life deeply hurt me. They say when you're not looking for a teacher, they will show up right in front of you. The problem is not everyone sees them standing there. Fortunately for me, I was looking for something, anything, that morning. I heard the church pastor talk about Resurrection week and how even broken people will be reborn this week. I knew at that very moment I was at the right place at the right time. Most people who know or know of me would tell you I have overcome astonishing odds. I would tell you that everyone has a story far greater and deeper than mine. I am just blessed to be breathing to share mine. I began to stand on my feet at my upper deck seat weeping and praying out loud to God. I have been delivered and blessed time and time again throughout my life. I've had my life spared when I should have practically died. To help you understand what I had been delivered from, I needed to take you down a road I wasn't always sure I would want to return to.

I once asked my mentor, "Why did all of this happen to my life?" His response was and always has been the same: "God was preparing you so that one day, you could teach others how to get through these great and unbearable odds of life." You know, everything in life is just a big puzzle. We don't know when it's happening to us; we only see the moment we are in.

What I've learned is that you must hold onto two things in life to be successful: where you are is not where you are going. Those two things have kept me alive all those years and continue today. Everyone reading this book has a story about their life. This was mine.

Made in the USA
Monee, IL
20 September 2023

43024007R00085